A CASEBOOK OF
OTHERWORLDLY
MUSIC

Other books by D. Scott Rogo

A Psychic Study of the Music of the Spheres
Methods and Models for Education in Parapsychology
The Welcoming Silence
An Experience of Phantoms
Parapsychology: A Century of Inquiry
In Search of the Unknown
Exploring Psychic Phenomena
The Haunted Universe
Mind Beyond the Body
Minds and Motion
The Haunted House Handbook
The Poltergeist Experience
Phone Calls from the Dead (with Raymond Bayless)
Earth's Secret Inhabitants (with Jerome Clark)
The Tujunga Canyon Contacts (with Ann Druffel)
UFO Abductions
Miracles
ESP and Your Pet
Leaving the Body
Our Psychic Potentials
The Search for Yesterday
Life after Death
Mind over Matter

A CASEBOOK OF OTHERWORLDLY MUSIC

VOL. 1 OF PARANORMAL MUSIC EXPERIENCES

BY D. SCOTT ROGO

ANOMALIST BOOKS
San Antonio • New York

NAD (nŏd): A Sanskrit term signifying transcendental, astral, psychic, or paranormal music—music heard from no apparent source. Also written NADA, the final A being silent.

Table of Contents

Chapter 1 NAD — Introduction 11

2 NAD and out-of-the-Body Travel 18

3 NAD in Normal States of Consciousness 35

4 NAD — Related to Death 51

5 NAD, Hauntings, and the Psychic Ether 73

6 NAD, Mystics, and Mediums 85

7 NAD — Some Further Cases 108

8 NAD and Its Relevancy to the Survival Issue 129

Postscript by Dr. Robert Crookall 147

Appendix A The Supreme Adventure: The Journey into Death 149

B A Survey of Literature on the out-of-the-Body Experience 157

Acknowledgments and Bibliography 171

Preface

I wish to acknowledge the assistance of the following people who aided in the preparation of this book: Mr. Raymond Bayless, who helped research case material and whose suggestions were most valuable; Mr. Maurice Barbanell and *Psychic News*, through which I was able to gather many of the personal accounts included; Dr. Robert Crookall, who kindly lent his counsel; Mr. and Mrs. Vincent Gaddis, who opened their files to me; Mrs. Winifred Rogo, who assisted in the preparation of the manuscript; and all those who sent their personal experiences to me with permission to insert them in this work.

Readers who have experienced the phenomenon of "Psychic Music" are invited to write me, giving full details of the incident.

D. SCOTT ROGO

7312 Beck Avenue
North Hollywood, California
91605

Chapter 1

NAD — Introduction

Professor Ernesto Bozzano was a singularly prolific writer, investigator, and theorist on parapsychological phenomena. But now that parapsychology has adopted the exactitudes of modern science and emphasizes a statistical appraisal of psychical phenomena, Bozzano has been forgotten. Yet those all too few students of the evolution of psychic science will ever revere him as one of the most important scholars and theorists in the history of the subject.

In his *A propos de l'Introduction à la Metapsychique* we find a synthesis of the various psychical phenomena which (in the view of Bozzano—a firm believer that psychical phenomena demonstrate that man survives bodily death) were best explained on a "spiritistic" hypothesis, which theorizes such occurrences as being the activity of the "dead." Many of these points still are to be found in parapsychological literature: apparitions at the moment of death, "bilocation," and the speaking in languages not normally known to the medium allegedly communicating with the "dead."

However, certain of Bozzano's points are now forgotten altogether —one such being "transcendental music" heard at deathbeds.

This last point must remain an enigma, for of all Bozzano's "intimations of immortality" (of which several others are indexed) this one seems to be, as is with most of his writings, one of those many scholarly enunciations which history has not honored. This, even though Bozzano gave such prominence to the phenomenon that no student of parapsychology could possibly overlook his preoccupation with it. Within recent years only continental authorities have felt the impact imparted by that Italian philosopher.

René Sudre, a seasoned parapsychologist, though an extreme negativist on survival, has in his *Treatise on Parapsychology* (Allen & Unwin, 1960) taken Bozzano to task on many theoretical issues. Sudre writes:

> Bozzano collected three groups of spontaneous cases which he regarded as inexplicable. These were apparitions of the deceased at a death-bed, telekinetic phenomena related to a death, and what he called "transcendental music."

While Sudre adequately, though not necessarily correctly, censures the first two of Bozzano's claims to a state of theoretical immobility (in their survivalistic implication) by quoting the standard antisurvivalist dicta,[1] his short analysis of "transcendental music" is a bit puzzling; for instead of offering a counter-solution to the phenomena, he offers no solution at all. Sudre states (page 346):

> These are auditory phenomena which are more easily produced by illusion than visual ones. . . . Before accepting so improbable a hypothesis as that of "choirs of angels," we must exhaust all the others, even that of pathological hallucinations. But an objective interpretation of such cases cannot be given unless the evidence is sufficiently reliable and detailed, which it often is not.

M. Sudre's position may be criticized sternly. While he readily points to seemingly hordes of counter-theories, which he refers to

---

[1] That both apparitions and telekinesis at death are "telepathic hallucinations." This author finds this explanation at variance with much collected data.

as "all the others," he certainly dulls his astuteness by not quoting even a sampling of them. Such an oversight is no accident, as any student of Sudre's carefully planned argumentation must be aware. While he offers us substitutions for Bozzano's other spontaneous death phenomena, Sudre's handling of music phenomena breaks his own argumentative consistency. Further, he qualifies his own negation of the objective reality of the experience by stating that positive evidence is "often" not detailed. Is this not implying that, in fact, such data does exist?

Where does this argument lead us? Unfortunately only within the limits of idle speculation. For it must be admitted that no volume has ever been presented which exclusively occupies itself with the problem of "psychic music."

While Sudre and Bozzano both studied the phenomenon with a bias for or against the survival of bodily death, they both overstepped the boundaries of their investigations. The reason is that it must be frankly admitted that even up to the present not enough is known about the phenomenon, its very existence, modus operandi, or forms even to speculate on its theoretical bearings.

The survival discussions of Sudre and Bozzano little concern the nature of this volume. For, in keeping with my statement that not enough data have been collected or analyzed on the subject, we will explore certain major problems confronting the theorist before any authoritative pronouncements may be made concerning the phenomenon. And the most important is very simply, "Does the phenomenon exist?" If we can verify this, our second question is, "What forms does it take?" And as a point of academic interest, "Is the phenomenon known in different cultures than our own?"

It is important to note that this phenomenon is not to be thought of as solely connected with death. As an analysis of case studies reveals (and will be presented "in toto" within the scope of this book), this phenomenon has been experienced by perfectly normal persons in normal states of consciousness. Mr. Raymond Bayless, a noted parapsychologist who has authored both a book and several papers on the paranormal, was one of the first to bring this eerie

13

phenomenon to my attention. It is all the more valuable that Mr. Bayless, as a teen-ager, had experienced this phenomenon, to which many have proffered the Pythagorean title "The Music of the Spheres." I quote his narrative in full (*in litt.* Dec. 9, 1968):

Case No. 1 — Raymond Bayless

One evening after I had gone to bed and was still awake and fully conscious (I was about thirteen years of age) I heard apparently in the distance the sound of what I believed to be a radio playing. At first the music—at the very beginning I realized that it was music I was hearing —was barely heard, but it steadily gained in volume until it was clearly and distinctly heard, and it then diminished until it faded out completely. It was impossible to estimate the duration of the incident but I would guess that no more than a few minutes actually passed. It was also impossible to locate the music in space.

Immediately the skeptic will raise an objection on the ground that the percipient of this case was the victim of a dream, a hallucination, or an acoustical freak. However, note the "other-worldness" of the second half of the narrative:

I was interested in music greatly, but at the time possessed no "formal" knowledge of type or origin. In spite of this lack, I became completely aware that the music was totally unearthly and inconceivably beautiful and majestic. The greatest music on earth, be it Brahms or Bach, is nothing but an inharmonious jangle of crude sounds by comparison. It was literally celestial and at the time I believed it to be associated with religious matters, and I still believe this to be so. It seemed to be produced by vast numbers of players, singers; I do not know, but the sense of a great number of units was felt. I cannot say that the music was vocal or that it was instrumental; it was on an inconceivably higher level than such distinction, and all that can be said is that it was incredibly beautiful, clearly

14

superhuman, and could not possibly originate from earthly instruments or voices. In spite of the time that has passed— I am almost forty-nine—, the memory of the experience is powerful and unforgettable.

Students of Roman Catholic mysticism will immediately see a relationship between this case and similar ones in the phenomenology of the saints. This factor brings us to a problem of categorization. Is the phenomenon a parapsychological one (such as recorded by Bozzano) or a religious one? Clearly the two overlap, since it is evident that our modern knowledge of psychical research is adaptable to the supernatural states exhibited in the lore of saints.[2] Apparently as Mr. Bayless's case in point reveals, the experience often has religious connotations. But again there are many instances where the phenomenon occurred collectively, that is, was heard simultaneously by a number of percipients, yet no religious connection was associated with it. (Several of these cases will be cited.)

Raymond Bayless's narrative is important in that (although he does not cite this extremely significant point in his report) the phenomenon was subjective—another person in the room having no reaction to the "mystical" transpiration. However, it is not to be assumed that the phenomenon was hallucinatory or even truly "subjective." To illustrate this point, we can invoke the dog whistle analogy. The sound has an objective reality, yet it is not audible to most human ears.

In order to construct a suitable category for this phenomenon, we can do no better than employ the phrase "other-world experience" to designate those weird paranormal events which seem to point to a higher physical reality; to a paranormal basis of human existence. Professor J. H. M. Whiteman, who makes clear use of this terminology,[3] has shown its deep parapsychological significance.

---

[2] Fr. Herbert Thurston: *The Physical Phenomena of Mysticism, Surprising Mystics.* Also, Montague Summers: *The Physical Phenomena of Mysticism.*

[3] J. H. M. Whiteman: "Evidence of Survival from 'Other-World' Experiences," *Journal* A.S.P.R., Vol. LIX, No. 2.

Since this is not a study in metaphysics, mysticism, or religion, but a book on psychical phenomena, it would be well worth our while to outline under what conditions the phenomenon precipitates. It is quite obvious that most of these categories have distinct psychical implications.

AWAKE
NORMAL

1. As we have already illustrated, the experience may appear to have no external agent and may be heard by persons in normal states.

Death

2. Secondly we have a complex network of cases connected with death: the dying hearing "celestial music," observers at deathbeds hearing strains of music—often collectively heard, and obviously telepathic cases in which music is heard by a percipient who immediately recognizes the music as being coincidental with a death of a friend or relative. While this last-mentioned genre appears to be telepathic, there are a few collective cases on record and these will be examined.

Out of
Body

3. Our next category is one which has both psychical and religious overtones—the "out-of-the-body" experience or "astral projection" in which the human consciousness appears to disconnect itself from the corporeal body and function independently of it, sometimes accompanied by a duplicate "apparition" body. Various astral travelers have heard celestial music. It is quite concordant that persons near death have described out-of-the-body experiences and also have simultaneously described hearing music.

Robert Crookall, who has authored no fewer than eight books on the subject of astral projection, has himself noted that "many people who suffered pseudo-death and many astral projectors state, quite independently of mediums, that they heard sweet sounds, and these they not unnaturally called 'music.' Many of those who have left the body permanently (the 'dead') make the same statement through mediums."[4]

HAUNTED

4. Of extreme interest are a few cases in which musical sounds

[4] Crookall, Robert, *Events on the Threshold of the After-Life* (Moradabad, India, Darshana International, 1967).

16

have been precipitated in so-called "haunted houses."

5. Our last category has clear religious implications, and may *Religious* also be listed under several subheadings: cases related to mystical persons (such as saints, ascetics, and yogi), musical sounds heard in the presence of "mediums," and religious documents which give theoretical discourse to divine music. In this last subsection we find the Tantric Yogic doctrine of NAD—superhuman music, and the term from which the title of this book was adopted.

Reviewing these categories, one realizes overtly that Ernesto Bozzano was quite correct in categorizing "transcendental music" as a clearly defined parapsychological concern. And this volume will be oriented in that direction.

Chapter 2

NAD and out-of-the-Body Travel

At the outset of this volume, I stated that we could classify the NAD as an "other-world" experience. Another phenomenon of this category is the out-of-the-body experience, also commonly known as "astral projection."

In order to avoid conjecture on whether the experience has a physical reality, I will use the initials OOBE in referring to the phenomenon at present.

Simply, the experience consists of the feeling that one is leaving the body and existing apart from it as a separate entity. Sometimes the newly released consciousness perceives itself enveloped in an "apparition" body—an exact replica of the physical body; and sometimes, though rarely, it may be perceived as an apparition by a percipient.[1]

A rather typical example of the phenomenon is the experience of Captain Burton (first published in J. Arthur Hill's *Man Is a Spirit*, Cassell & Co., Ltd., 1918):

---

[1] There are several such cases in *Phantasms of the Living*, a two-volume collection of spontaneous cases published in 1886. The authors were Edmund Gurney, F. W. H. Myers, and Frank Podmore, all of whom were instrumental in founding the Society for Psychical Research (1882).

I had heart failure. I found myself standing at the foot of my bed, looking at myself and the doctor and feeling very well and bright, though puzzled. Then suddenly I found myself dragged violently over the bed rail where I floated above myself; following which came a tremendous crash. Then I heard the doctor's voice: "He is coming round." He had considered me dead for some time.

The literature on this subject is voluminous (see Appendix B) and while it has been suggested that the phenomenon is a hallucination, there are numerous cases in which the projector was able to travel and return to the body with (ostensibly) paranormal veridical information about a distant place.

The most important work in this field has been done by Dr. Robert Crookall, late principal Geologist, H. M. Geological Survey; and formerly Demonstrator in Botany, University of Aberdeen. In 1961 Robert Crookall published *The Study and Practice of Astral Projection* (London, Aquarian Press) which recorded one hundred and sixty cases of OOBEs, some from preexisting sources, others never before appearing in print. In 1964 a sequel was forthcoming, *More Astral Projections* (London, Aquarian Press), which compiled two hundred and twenty-two further cases, many received by its author *in litt.*

Robert Crookall's work has many distinctions which, taken collectively, reveal the phenomenon to be a genuine psychical concern. The phenomenon often occurs at moments when a person is close to death, during illness, as a reaction to anesthesia, and sometimes in perfectly (ostensibly) normal states.

Robert Crookall's first distinction is having presented, en masse, over three hundred cases. His second contribution is pointing out the intercorroboration between various accounts. Basically, this manner of analyzing testimony is based on the words of Archbishop Richard Whately:

When many coincide in their testimony (where no previous concert can have taken place), the probability resulting from this concurrence does not rest upon the supposed veracity of each considered separately, but on the improbability of such an agreement taking place by chance. For, though in such a case each of the witnesses should be unworthy of credit, still, the chances would be infinite against their all agreeing in the same falsehood. [*The Law of Evidence*, 1865].

In the case of those claiming OOBEs, we do have several cases in which independent persons have described common experiences. Professor Hornell Hart, a prime parapsychologist, has maintained that Dr. Crookall's work has presented four additional "lines of proof" ("*A Chasm Needs to be Bridged,*" *Journal* A.S.P.R., Volume 60, No. 4):

1. That, as already stated, all the cases seem to fall into a basic pattern: the patterns which are described in Appendix I of *More Astral Projections*. These include: feeling that the consciousness is leaving through the head; floating above the physical body, usually from a few inches to a few feet above; seeing the physical body from a point in space outside the body; seeing the "astral" body connected to the physical body via a luminous cord (usually described as "silver" in color); immunity to the obstruction of physical objects; usually invisible, though sometimes viewed as an agent in an apparitional experience; sometimes seeing other "astral bodies" of the (presumably) "dead" or "permanently projected." (In a good number of cases, persons have stated that they have been aided in projection by "discarnates." Crookall has gone into this matter more fully in *During Sleep* [Theosophical Publishing House, 1964].)

After these general experiences is a list of highly specific occurrences often encountered: the feeling of being drawn through a tunnel; a "black-out" at the time of exit and reentry into the physical body; hearing clicking sounds at times of exit or reentry; "spiraling" out of the body; and so on.

2. There appear to be similar records in all periods of history

and in different cultures. For example, within the scope of his two published case books, Dr. Crookall has included records of OOBEs from Tibet (Case No. 82), Ancient China (No. 83), Iceland (No. 22), American Indians (Nos. 208, 255), Gold Coast natives (No. 210), India (No. 213), Siberia (No. 305), and elsewhere.

3. Several cases are narratives of children of such early age as to make it highly unlikely that they had ever heard of such a phenomenon from which to model their accounts. Secondly, many contributors have claimed no prior knowledge of the phenomenon before their own experiences.

4. The fourth point is perhaps Dr. Crookall's most important contribution to the field: OOBEs are roughly separated into two categories, "natural" (in a normal state of health, ill, exhausted, near death) and "enforced" (caused by anesthetics, suffocation, falling, or hypnosis). Dr. Crookall has pointed out that the "patterns" intrinsic to OOBE accounts differ substantially between natural and enforced cases, yet are concordant to each other in their classification, and generally fit the patterns to which all OOBEs are subject.

This discovery is detailed in Appendix I of *More Astral Projections*, in which two hundred and fourteen "natural" cases (N) and thirty-seven "enforced" (EN) are examined. Of the N cases 13.5 percent described leaving through the head as opposed to only 5.4 percent of the EN cases. During N cases the "double" was initially in a horizontal position 23.3 percent, while EN cases revealed 18.9 percent. The ratio of doubles returning to the physical body in a horizontal position was 3.2 percent (N) to 0 (EN). In those cases where a rapid return to the physical body caused shock or repercussion to the physical body, we have 10.7 percent in N cases to 5.4 percent in EN.

Furthermore, the "permanently projected" were seen in 22.6 percent of N cases to 16.2 percent for EN cases. One outstanding difference is the relationship between instances wherein the level of consciousness was "supernormal"; 22.6 percent N to only 5.4 percent EN.

Out-of-the-body travelers have several times contacted different types of environments. Several mention that they were still in an earth-environment 31.0 percent (N) to 78.4 percent (EN). Some have reported reaching a "paradise" condition: 14.5 percent (N) to but a mere 2.7 percent (EN). In a third category are those who found themselves, after leaving the body, enveloped by a misty world or "hades" condition—only 1.8 percent in the natural projections to 5.4 percent in the enforced.

The differences between N and EN cases are considerable. Dr. Crookall has shown in a recent volume, *Events on the Threshold of the Afterlife* (1967, Darshana International), that N cases usually describe the cord as being connected between the heads of the two "bodies," while a notable number of EN cases depict this cord as stemming from the solar plexus of the physical body. Even a few have seen two cords issuing from both the head and the solar plexus (Case No. 364, for example).

When these data are collected and classified, it is hard to dismiss OOBEs as mere hallucination. Recently Dr. Charles Tart of the University of California at Davis has presented two papers which indicate that the OOBE can be registered by an electroencephalograph (brain wave recording device) and other psychophysiological testing apparatus (see Appendix B). This certainly augments the pioneering work of Robert Crookall.

The reader may wonder why such prominence has been given to a phenomenon that at first would appear far removed from the central theme of this book, NAD—transcendental music. A priori, it would seem to me that having classified NAD as an "other-world" experience, some relationship should be found between it and the OOBE, another "other-world" experience. This has been borne out in reviewing several cases in which the narrators of OOBEs note the hearing of "psychic" music.

Case No. 2 — M. E. Henley

The first case (from *Psychic News*, June 4, 1955) appears to be a form of OOBE. Bracketed remarks are mine.

Forty years ago [when the subject was twenty] on a bright June night I was lying in bed wide awake. [Several cases of OOBE occur at this time.] To my surprise a wide crack appeared in the ceiling: It widened and the two halves rolled away to the sides of the room. The roof parted in the same way and I clearly saw the sky. Then the voice of an old friend, who had died several years before, said, just as he used to speak to me, "Come child." Though I saw no one, my hand was clasped and I rose from my bed up through the roof [being "guided" has been described in many OOBEs]. *Then I was in a large building filled with beautiful music.* Again the voice said, "Come, child," and I found myself back in bed, tears streaming down my face as I pleaded to be allowed to return with my old friend.

Robert Crookall, who used this case (No. 215), wrote to Mrs. Henley and quotes her as stating that she had no previous knowledge of the subject. She also made note of other OOBEs, including feeling the "pull" of the "cord" at the back of the head (a fairly common observation). When all these factors are catalogued, in spite of the initial grandeur of such an experience, it does, when stripped to its bare essentials, fit fairly well into the pattern of many OOBEs.

Case No. 3 — S. H. Kelley

Another case taken from Crookall is that of S. H. Kelley (Southport, England) recounted as Case No. 343 in *More Astral Projections* (Aquarian Press, 1964).

S. H. Kelley's narrative tells of his having an OOBE during a swimming exercise in which he almost drowned: "I started to swim back, got cramp and could not move arms or legs. . . . As I lost consciousness, certain things in my life came in front of me. [This is often stated by persons close to death. See Crookall *The Supreme Adventure,* James Clarke, 1961.] *This was followed by a queer sound of music* and the next thing I [double] was suspended in midair and looking at them bringing my body out of the water, and

23

trying artificial respiration. I was freer and happy. . . . Why were they doing that when I was here?"

At this point Mr. Kelley found himself transported to his mother's room, but soon found himself back again by his body. "A brilliant light shone around me and a voice said 'it is not your time yet—you must go back, you have work to do.' [This "command" is not unique in OOBE lore.] Immediately I began to come down to my body and the lads around it. Then everything was dark [the "blackout" effect] and my eyes opened. They all said, 'He's alive.' I got up and went back to the hut, with everyone amazed."

We may note in this case several points suggestive of other OOBE cases: floating above the body, the command to reenter the body, the blackout effect, and the "flashback" noted by many persons having OOBEs who are near death.

Case No. 4 — Kathleen Snowden

A third case quoted from Crookall (Case No. 339, from the same source as above) is almost a "typical" case of OOBE: including such experiences as floating toward a "golden light"[2] and the distaste for having to return to the physical body, which is a mental state almost universally applicable to those describing OOBEs.

> I was only sixteen years old, ill in bed, I told mother I thought I was going to faint . . . I felt myself drifting away from her. Suddenly I realized a feeling of great excitement, wonder, and delight surpassing anything I had ever experienced as I felt my body [double] weightless and floating upwards in a golden glow towards a wonderful light around hazy welcoming figures *and the whole air was filled with beautiful singing.*
>
> I floated joyfully towards the voices and the light and

---

[2] Mr. Raymond Bayless has drawn my attention to a painting by the Flemish master H. Bosch, which depicts "souls" traveling toward a light-filled tunnel in the sky. This is most suggestive of OOBE cases in which the subject tells of such a gleaming tunnel.

then I heard my mother's voice calling me. . . . My whole being revolted against going back. Her voice grew nearer and to my great distress, I felt myself slipping away from that wonderful light and merging into a dull black cloud where my heaviness of body returned. . . . My mother thought I had died; I had seemed to stop breathing. . . . I am now forty-two and the wonder of it still remains.

The reader will note that in both the last two cases cited the NAD was perceived in a very similar fashion.

Case No. 5 — Prescott Hall

The case of Prescott Hall (*Journal* A.S.P.R. Volume X, 1916) is of extreme interest. Hall had been the recipient of a quantity of "spirit teachings" through the mediumship of Mrs. Minnie Keeler, which dealt not only with the doctrine of the "astral body" but actual methods of projecting it. (The techniques are quite remarkable and have been discussed by Robert Crookall in detail in *Techniques of Astral Projection* [Aquarian Press, 1964].) Prescott Hall attempted to project his own double over a period of six years. During his experiments, Hall made such indicative comments as "feeling of being drawn out of the body . . . feeling of being pulled out. [October 7, 8, 10, 1909]." A propos to NAD, Hall recorded (September 3, 1909), "Sense of physical body falling down and away. Definite feeling that I am not in my body—*faint music*." On March 13, 1910, Hall described a "snap" (the significance of which I have already mentioned), and "then a great yellowish light above me [compare to the previous case of the "golden-glow"] . . . *a new musical sound.*"[3]

Case No. 6 — James C. Edgerton

This case (taken from Sylvan Muldoon's *The Case for Astral*

---

[3] By following the Keeler methods on diet control, I had two spontaneous OOBEs in 1965. The records are in the possession of Drs. Crookall and Tart.

Projection, Aries Press, 1946, 2d ed.) was caused by anesthetics (ether):

> On the second breath [of ether], an unusual train of circumstances started which can best be described by the statement that my physical senses suddenly seemed to shift into a body other than the physical, with no mental lapse whatsoever, I was clearly conscious that I was sitting up and that my eyes seemed to take on X-ray qualities which reduced my physical body to a mere shadow with the ankle and knee joints slightly more than prominent.
>
> I saw another body within this shell, glistening brilliantly, and as I watched this new body of which I seemed to be a part, and which was more objective to me than my physical body had ever been, I slid out of my fleshy envelope with rapidly increasing acceleration. During this interval my other senses were also functioning, the sense of feeling being concerned with a soul-shaking wrench which seemed to extend to every cell of my body.
>
> *To my ears came a beautiful sine wave note, corresponding to middle E on the piano, which increased from zero to volume which seemed to fill the universe.* Following this I heard a voice which I seemed to respond to as to any physical voice which repeated these words. "You are now suffering all the pangs of violent death. You are in the hands of friends and everything will be all right." I did not lose consciousness until I was entirely separate from the physical body [blackout], which I knew beyond any question I had left.

Note in this case the comment that the music "increased from zero to volume which seemed to fill the universe." Compare this to Raymond Bayless (Case No. 1), who states very similarly: "At first the music was barely heard, but it steadily gained in volume until it was clearly and distinctly heard, and then it diminished until it faded out completely." As further cases are cited, some other narratives will note this crescendo effect of the music.

Case No. 7 — Mrs. Emma Powell

Mrs. Powell's case was sent to me on tape by her grandson, Mr. Louis Nelson, who had described her experience to me. On the tape, received November, 1968, Mrs. Powell stated:

> I had an out-of-the-body experience in 1926 in November. My daughter was a baby, I had been ill but was out of bed and doing pretty well. But this night, I lay down to go to sleep and I left my body and went straight up, very slowly, *but all the time I could hear music and the higher I got the louder the music became. It was the most beautiful music I have ever heard.* But I could hear my baby crying and it seemed like she was a way, way off, and I asked the Lord to let me come back, she needed me [quite often OOBEs have terminated when the agent feels a concern over a still living relative who would suffer by the death]. And instantly I was back in my body, and then I could feel my mother and father's hands working with me and saying that I was cold and that they could hardly find a pulse. I knew I had been close to Heaven or another world.

I wrote to Mrs. Powell and, in response to my questions, she stated that the music appeared to emanate from a point above her. The occurrence happened at 8:30 p.m. She established the fact that she had no formal knowledge of the phenomenon by writing, "I had other experiences before the above-mentioned experience, but had never heard of psychic phenomena."

Case No. 8 — L. Opfolter-Hull

In response to a letter in *Psychic News* in which I simply requested readers to send any experiences concerning hearing "astral music," Mrs. L. Opfolter-Hull sent me (in litt. Nov. 8, 1968) the story of her grandmother's encounter. Note the similarity between this account and that of Mrs. Powell [Case No. 7]:

When a young girl in India, in the '20's, my grandmother, then a woman in her 60's, told me of her experience just after giving birth to my mother; of floating up towards the most *beautiful choir* she had ever heard. She longed to go on until she found the choir, but her baby drew her back. She had always loved harmonizing human voices, and would stop and listen whenever she heard them, but that particular choir at her baby's birth was the most lovely—and unearthly.

Case No. 9 — Miss A. M. H.

A very interesting and complex case that is actually an instance in which the music was collectively heard was originally recorded in Robert Owen's *Footfalls on the Boundary of Another World* (Trubner, 1860).

Miss A. M. H., not knowing that her friend "S." was ill, had a "dream" in which she found herself in "S.'s" house. She writes, "There, on the bed, I saw 'S.' as if about to die. I walked up to him, and, filled with hope, said, 'You are not going to die. Be comforted. You will live.' As I spoke *I seemed to hear an exquisite strain of music sounding through the room.*" After "waking," Miss A. M. H. and her mother dispatched a letter to "S." inquiring about his state of health. By return post, it was verified that "S." had been seriously ill.

Three years later Miss A. M. H. and her mother chanced to meet "S." in London and thereupon Miss A. M. H. recounted her dream. "S." then claimed that he had tried to encourage his brother to send for her, but that the brother had dissuaded him. During his illness he had seen her phantom and *"I would also hear my favorite sonata by Beethoven. . . . You walked up to the bed with a cheerful air, and, while the music which I longed for filled the air,* spoke to me encouragingly, saying I should not die."

If indeed this was actually a reciprocal telepathically produced apparition, and not an OOBE, then it goes far beyond any data we presently have for such theories. Such cases of music heard at death-

28

beds shall be covered extensively in another section of this volume, and have many characteristics of being objective.

Case No. 10 — Mrs. E. Hatfield

This case, received *in litt.* by Robert Crookall, constitutes his Case No. 123 (*The Study and Practice of Astral Projection*, Aquarian Press, 1961; University Books Inc., 1966). Note the "tunnel effect," the movement toward a light, and the command to reenter the body —all of which have been mentioned previously.

> In 1927, I was given ether. I seemed to float down a dark tunnel, moving towards a half-moon of light that was miles away. *I heard the sound of music* and smelled the scent as of an old-fashioned bouquet. Then my flight down the tunnel was halted, although there was no obstruction; I could not go further. I staged a rebellion. I wanted to go on. A voice said, "Go back and live." Then I found myself back in the body. I am convinced that I was dead to this world but wholly alive to another.

Case No. 11 — Gertrude Snow-Palmer

Again I find myself drawing from the published records of Dr. Robert Crookall. This one (Case No. 158 from the same source) is extremely lengthy and will be abridged.

Mrs. Palmer, who claimed no previous knowledge of the phenomenon, had this experience during an illness:

> I became aware of an odd sensation that started at my feet and progressed slowly upwards past my hips and began to affect my abdomen, and I began to understand that I was dying . . . the sensation travelled swiftly up past my arms and when it went into my head, I was suddenly not in my body, but above it. I was even above the roof of the house, which became as if it were not there—it was transparent— There was no feeling of having a body of any kind. . . . First

29

I noticed my seven-year-old son, playing with blocks. Then my attention was drawn to a far-away brightness that called me mightily. The atmosphere that I inhabited in this state was a lovely pink haze. [This is typical of many narratives.] *There was also a swelling of beautiful music something like a pipe-organ.* . . . I looked back. . . . I could see my physical body lying there. At the same time I saw my husband coming up the walk and I knew he would be terrified if he found my body lifeless down there. I didn't want to go back, but I knew I must and then I was back. . . . I don't know how long it was before I got my eyes opened, but when I did I was satisfied that going back was the only thing I could do.

Mrs. Palmer notes that upon reentering her body she felt cataleptic, which is again a common feature of these experiences.

Case No. 12 — Doyle's Correspondent

While cases such as these have been forgotten by parapsychologists, Sir Arthur Conan Doyle put significant stock in them. He quotes a correspondent as writing of an experience, "It was the most vivid and beautiful dream [obviously the agent had no knowledge of the OOBE, though she stumbles onto the general concept at the end of her letter] I have ever experienced. When I came to myself I thought that if death was like that I should not mind going at any time [a common attitude]. Is it then possible for the soul to leave the body for a short time and return again?" (From *Edge of the Unknown*, Putnam, 1930.)

Doyle himself fills in the missing parts of the letter: "She lay at the point of death with a temperature of 105°. She was insensible but dreaming [Doyle probably had little knowledge of OOBE] vividly. *She seems to hear music of unearthly beauty* and to be surrounded by the faces of many loved ones who had passed on."

This is all highly evidential. Many persons having OOBEs describe seeing dead relatives. Further the "dead" themselves have stated (communicating through mediums) that they had been met by their own relatives and friends. (Crookall details this in *The Supreme Adventure*.) Further, Sir William Barrett in his little book *Death-bed Visions*, published over forty years ago, shows the bearing such cases (seeing deceased relatives at the point of death) have on psychical research. Recently Dr. Karlis Osis, presently the Research Officer of the American Society for Psychical Research, issued a monograph, published by the Parapsychology Foundation, *Deathbed Observations by Physicians and Nurses* (Parapsychological Monograph No. 3, 1961). On a few occasions these phantoms have been seen by visitors at deathbeds.

Case No. 13 — J. W. Skelton

This incident where an OOBE included hearing psychic music dates to 1890. Originally printed in the *Proceedings* of the S.P.R. Volume XI, page 560, it was included by F. W. H. Myers in his monumental *Human Personality and Its Survival of Bodily Death*. The cause of the OOBE seems to be related to no specific cause:

> I was engaged with two other men one day about two o'clock p.m. in taking out some evergreen trees from a box car to take home and set out; they were large and heavy— just at that instant I saw a medium-sized person standing at my right hand, clothed in white with a bright countenance, beaming with intelligence. I knew what he wanted in an instant, although he put his hand on my shoulder and said, "Come with me." We moved upward and a little to the southeast with the speed of lightning [this type of locomotion is constantly referred to in cases such as this].... As we passed on, this glorious being that was with me told me he was going to show me that bright heavenly world. We came to a world of light and beauty.... I saw many thousand spirits clothed in white, *and singing heavenly music— the sweetest song I have ever heard.*

Mr. Skelton went on to say that he saw the "spirits" of his deceased mother, two sisters, and child, but was not allowed to con-

31

verse with them. Many astral travelers claim to visit deceased relatives, and quite a few spontaneous OOBEs report this. He said his "guide" told him "We must go back." He said, "I wished to stay but he told me my time had not come yet, but would in due time and that I should wait with patience."

On recovering his senses and checking his watch, he calculated that the experience had lasted twenty-six minutes.

> One of the men said, "there is something the matter with you ever since you opened the car door; we have not been able to get a word out of you!" and that I had done all the work of taking out everything and putting it back into the car, and one item was eight barrels of flour I had taken off the ground alone and put back in the car, three feet and a half high, with all the ease of a giant.

Case No. 14 — Rosamond Lehmann

I shall close this section of cases with a rather odd account which originally appeared in *Light*, Summer, 1962.

Miss Rosamond Lehmann, apparently emotionally shattered by the death of her daughter, experienced several psychic occurrences, among which was an OOBE. While in this state, she heard what she described as an awesome outburst of symphonic music. She noted that no radio was playing at the time and that the house in which she experienced the NAD was rather abandoned in a glen. Further, the English authoress noted that the music *swelled in intensity and then seemed to ebb*. The music itself seemed familiar but she could not recognize it.

There are three regularities within these reports which deserve special attention. In no case (with the possible exception of that from Robert Dale Owen) was the music recognized. In most cases the percipients described it simply as beyond earthly construction, or at least intensely beautiful. Mrs. Henley said of it, "beautiful music"; Kathleen Snowden described it as "beautiful singing"; Mrs.

Powell, "the most beautiful music I have ever heard"; Mrs. Opfolter-Hull reported that the music was "the most beautiful choir" she had "ever heard"; Miss A. M. H. called it "an exquisite strain of music"; while Mrs. Palmer called it "a swelling of beautiful music." Doyle's correspondent designated it as "music of unearthly beauty"; while yet another, J. W. Skelton, who *saw* the music being sung, referred to it as "heavenly music." Rosamond Lehmann labels her experience with a group of colorful adjectives.

The reader will note that all the above cases from which I quoted are *natural* out-of-the-body cases. In analyzing *enforced* OOBEs, wherein music was perceived, we discover a totally different group of descriptions which would very well fit in with Dr. Robert Crookall's discovery that natural and enforced cases have strong experiential differences. S. H. Kelley, who had an OOBE when he nearly drowned, unenthusiastically describes "a queer sound of music"; Prescott Hall, trying artificially to project himself, heard only "faint music"; James Edgerton under ether heard only "a beautiful wave note"; and Mrs. Hatfield, also under ether, heard only "the sound of music."

On a statistical level, natural cases reveal 100 percent who described the music in a superlative tone, while enforced cases show only 20 percent. This would fit in with Crookall's observation that persons in a natural OOBE have a higher level of consciousness.[4]

Another feature of these narratives is that many natural projectors have described the music as choral, while enforced projectors usually only stated hearing music. While some natural OOBE cases heard NAD as orchestral, the majority heard it as "singing."

Another important observation is the many references made to the crescendo effect of the music. Mrs. Powell recorded "the higher I got, the louder the music became." Mrs. Palmer states that the music "swelled," and Mrs. Lehmann writes that the music swelled

---

[4] This gives us a ratio of five to one. Crookall has shown that the consciousness was "supernormal" in N and EN cases at a ratio of four to one.

in intensity and then ebbed. James C. Edgerton (an enforced case) heard the NAD "increase from zero to volume which seemed to fill the Universe." We have already mentioned Mr. Bayless's account in which the sound grew and then faded away.

We can see that, just as with the OOBE, the NAD is equally controlled by similarly recurrent patterns. Also note that these patterns are quite often parallel to those experiences guiding natural and enforced projections. Such interconcordance is a prime issue in substantiating both the OOBE and NAD as objective phenomena.

Chapter 3

NAD in Normal States of Consciousness

We now come to one of the most important studies of this volume —NAD perceived by individuals in what would seem to be perfectly normal states of consciousness. And for the first time it appears that we will be studying the phenomenon as an entirely individual "other-world" experience. However, it can not be expected that any single phenomenon would be divorced from other data of similar phenomena. And this is true with NAD, as it is easy to maintain that many cases, while their percipients made no mention of the OOBE, occured in conditions where a quantitative examination of OOBE cases indicates that an OOBE *could have* taken place. In other words, the NAD occurs in conditions where enough OOBEs have been recorded that a causal relation may be designated.

Many of the following cases were sent to the author *in litt.* and oftentimes are not sufficiently detailed to allow a thorough analysis. However, since pure bulk is necessary to validate the phenomenon, I have included some rather brief accounts. Italicized print has been supplied in order to emphasize points of coincidence with other cases. Bracketed sections are my comments. No changes have been made in the cases sent *in litt.*, with the exception that irrelevant sections of the letters have been deleted and some grammatical changes have been made to insure greater readability.

Case No. 15 — Carl J. Barnes

The case of Mr. Barnes was originally published in *Fate* magazine (July, 1951):[1]

> In 1945 while flying at 6,000 feet near Sioux City, Iowa, for a period of thirty seconds I heard, or more exactly I felt, strains of the most fantastic music, *the like of which I have never heard before or since.* I remember thinking as the feeling passed that, if man could write and play such music, then more than mice of Hamelin town could be lured to some river's edge.
>
> The bomber was flying a routine training cruise. The radio operator sat at his position signaling ground station. I was lying on the radio room floor with my head on a parachute, when the melody floated into my consciousness. *The tune rose and fell and swelled in pitch and tone.* No sharp notes were struck and *no musical instruments ever heard could have made such a sound.*

Mr. Barnes goes on to compare the music to "the music of the spheres" and states that his radio operator heard "the strangest music."

High-altitude flying, which seems to have induced this case, has also been known to induce OOBEs. William T. Richardson has written (*Journal* S.P.R., 1961, p. 214), "Dissociation of mind with the physical world is apparently a fairly common phenomenon experienced by pilots, particularly those who fly at great heights and speeds. This sensation of 'out-of-body' is a momentary experience of detachment, a glimpse of one's self as though from without." Mr. Richardson subsequently quotes his own experience.

---

[1] All material used from *Fate* magazine appearing in this book has been reprinted by special permission of the publishers.

It might be thought that somehow this music was merely the plane's radio system picking up commercial broadcasting. Such cases are known and have been recorded (for example, during the Apollo 7 space flight). This music was found to be radio frequency interference coming from broadcast stations operating on frequencies with harmonics in the same frequency range as the spacecraft communications system. Also, such music was identified as sounding like commercial broadcasting.[2]

The above-quoted case cannot be explained by this or similar explanations in that: (1) the music was identified as "supernatural"; (2) it was not heard but "felt"; (3) two percipients heard the music, but in different forms (in the chapter on objective music heard at deathbeds, this phenomenon will be repeated); (4) notice also the comment that the music "swelled"; this is so similar to music heard during OOBEs that some relationship must be thought to exist.

Case No. 16 — A "Mystic"

In response to the above-cited case, one correspondent wrote to *Fate* (November-December, 1951): "I remember something told to me by one of my friends who is a mystic. Often she rises in the early morning, before the sun is up, to listen to this very music. She says it is most glorious harmony." Similar to Raymond Bayless's account (Case No. 1), this correspondent quotes her friend as relating the experience to religious matters.

Case No. 17 — Grace Russell

During a correspondence in which Miss Russell (Edmonds, Washington) was recounting a group of seemingly paranormal experiences to the author, she spontaneously wrote on October 15, 1968 (not knowing that I was working on a study of such cases): *"Once*

---

[2] I am indebted to the National Aeronautics and Space Administration (NASA) Houston, Texas, for these particulars.

I heard beautiful music coming from nowhere, divine music. It came from the air above me in *early morning*—a thousand violins; a thousand flutes, but really I could never say. It was just beautiful music, more beautiful than any I had ever heard."

I wrote to Miss Russell asking for a full account, and I quote from her letter of October 24, 1968:

It was very early one summer's morning that I heard the music. I had, if memory serves me, slept very soundly, as was usual with me. But suddenly I was awake and there was music, wonderful music, coming in through the only open window in the room. [This is at variance with the previous statement that the music emanated from a point just above her.] This room was on the first floor of a small house. Others in the house were asleep. All was quiet within. I got up, went to the window, and knelt before it looking into the morning light. I saw the large house across the way, perhaps fifty feet away. A widow and her daughter lived in this house. Neither cared for music. The music could not have come from there. It came from the air outside the window. It poured in, seemingly against my face as though some of the musicians were as close as ten feet from me—or so it seemed at the time and so it seems in memory.

I felt spellbound. I did not try to move. But I listened, and this is what I heard: *A very large group of instruments being played in a way I had never heard music played before.* It was as though the instruments were not far apart, but close together, at least that is the impression that I got.

I have thought about this music with sincere effort, trying to decide what instruments must have played it, but I have never come to a conclusion other than I did not know then and do not now. No one instrument played solo at any time. All played in unison. All played as one. But I felt there were many because of the variety of tones. *There were no wild clashes of sound, no beating of drums, no shrill high tones.* [Compare this to the statement of Mr. Barnes that

38

"no sharp tones were struck."] But there was definite melody, wonderful harmony. Back of the melody, which seemed an endless song without words, *I heard a deep roaring sound, something like the ocean's roar.* [This is similar to some experiences of exteriorization in OOBEs.] This was not louder than the rest, but it was there. The melody seemed to be carried by a *great* many instruments of high pitch expertly played. This music was of an intensity most unusual. It had meaning and great beauty. Not charm as some music but beauty that enthralled me.

This music seemed to come from many instruments; how many I hesitate to guess—*maybe hundreds.* [Compare to similar statements.] *First the music was soft and to the right of me, then louder, much louder.* I seemed to face it as it passed the window. It was strongest then. Then it came from the left, constantly growing softer. *It came from farther and farther and higher and higher until it died away.*

Miss Russell stated also that the experience lasted for about four minutes. It took place during a period of emotional depression, a mental state quite inducive to OOBEs.

Case No. 18 — Bayard Taylor

Not only has depression caused OOBEs, but sincere contemplative thought has also led up to some unique out-of-the-body experiences. This case comes to us from the author Bayard Taylor (1825-78), who, besides writing two books, translated an authoritative version of Goethe's *Faust.* This case is included in W. F. Prince's *Noted Witnesses for Psychic Occurrences* (reprint, University Books, 1963) and is quite detailed:

It was, perhaps, an hour past midnight, along the foothills of the Nevadas, when, as I lay with open eyes gazing into the eternal beauty of night, *I became conscious of a deep murmuring sound, like that of a rising wind.* [Compare to Miss Russell's "roaring ocean."] I looked at the trees; every branch was unmoved—*yet the sound was increased,* until the air of the lonely dell seemed to vibrate with its burden. A strange feeling of awe and expectancy took possession of me. Not a dead leaf stirred on the boughs; while the mighty sound—choral hymn, sung by *ten thousand voices*—swept down over the hills, and rolled away like retreating thunder over the plains. It was no longer the roar of the wind. As in the wandering prelude of an organ melody, note trod upon note with slow, majestic footsteps, until they gathered to a theme, and then came in the words, simultaneously chanted by an immeasurable host, *Vivant terrestria!* The air was filled with the tremendous sound, which seemed to sweep near the surface of the earth in powerful waves, without echo or reverberation.

Suddenly, far overhead, in the depths of the sky, rang a single, clear, piercing voice of unnatural sweetness—beyond the reach of human organs, or any human instrument, its keen alto piercing the firmament like a straight white line of electric fire. As it shot downward, gathering in force, *the vast terrestrial chorus gradually dispersed into silence,* and only that one unearthly sound remained. It vibrated slowly into the fragment of a melody, unlike any which had ever reached my ears—long undulating cry of victory and of joy, while the words *"Vivant Coelum!"* were repeated more and more faintly as the voice slowly withdrew, like a fading beam of sunset, into the abysses of the stars. Then all was silent. I was undeniably awake at the time, and could recall neither fact, reflection, nor fancy of a nature to suggest the sounds. . . . How does the faculty of the brain act, so far beyond our conscious knowledge, as to astound us with the most unexpected images? Why should it speak in the Latin tongue? How did it compose music—which would be as impossible for me as to write a Sanskrit poem?

Case No. 19 — A Swiss Boy

While Bayard Taylor's experience seems to be one of those rare cases in which actual words could be distinguished, similar experiences have been recorded. This next case, from Aniela Jaffe's *Apparitions and Precognition* (University Books, 1963), at first reads as though it were an instance of clairaudience (the audible version of clairvoyance) but was collectively perceived. Dr. Jaffe prefaces the account by writing: "A Swiss living in Russia tells how his fourteen-year-old son set out one night with a friend to a nearby brook to catch crayfish, and how they suddenly heard a confused singing which they soon recognized as a church choir."

> *Then all of a sudden the singing was all around us,* so that we could not tell whether it came from below, from side to side, or from above. After a while we could hear the priest's voice quite distinctly, then the choir chimed in again, singing antiphonally, as they do in the Orthodox Church.

Dr. Jaffe notes that this incident took place in Soviet Russia, where religious indoctrinations are discouraged.

Case No. 20 — P. B. Rowe

Mr. Rowe's short account (November 10, 1968) was written in reply to my letter in *Psychic News*. It read:

> I have experienced celestial music in my bedroom shortly after retiring. . . . I felt it was a choir's song around my bed and the music was wonderful.

This brief statement has two significant points. First, the case took place after retiring. This is concordant with many other reports where the experience was described as occurring shortly after retiring or upon waking. Needless to say, OOBEs are usually recorded at this time. Secondly, note that Mr. Rowe heard the music enveloping him. While this detail is at variance with several accounts which fix the music as emanating from a fixed point in space, other narrators have expressed the feeling that they were so encompassed.

41

Case No. 21 — Barbara Haslam

This case was received by the author on November 19, 1968, from Chatham, England, and reads:

> I awoke from sleep on the morning of May 19, 1965, at about 5 a.m. I lay there on my bed awake, and then *I heard a lovely horn sounding, starting low then going higher.* [Compare this to Case No. 6.], this happened three times; then *choral singing* with lovely music started, *the nicest I have ever heard.* It did not last for long, I should say about two minutes or so. I am sorry I do not know what they were playing and singing; *it seemed just above me* in the room.

In answer to a subsequent inquiry, Mrs. Haslam related the experience to religious matters.

Case No. 22 — Mrs. G.

One correspondent (November 10, 1968), who declined to give her name, sent a brief note stating that she had heard the music in 1967 and that it was choral music, quite loud, and that it would last until three or four in the morning.

Case No. 23 — Edgar Gooder

On November 7, 1968, Mrs. Mabel Gooder sent me a letter stating that her husband had heard "the celestial choir of thousands of voices" singing the word "Jerusalem" and the Hosannah.

In reply to an inquiry, Mr. Gooder wrote that the music emanated from a fixed point and that it had lasted for a duration of three minutes. He also stated that he could not remember ever having heard of the phenomenon before. It was mentioned that he had experienced an OOBE.

Case No. 24 — Elsie Haines

Mrs. Haines's report (in a letter dated November 7, 1968, Surrey, Great Britain) is of considerable importance since it occurred when she was a child, which, as we have noted with OOBEs, is a strong indication of the validity of the phenomenon (as Hart pointed out):

> I am delighted to say that I had a wonderful experience of waking up to the sound of full orchestra and very loud choir music when I was only about twelve years old. I had overslept on a Saturday morning (1921) and it was about 10 a.m. I felt very shocked and went to the window still hearing the music and saw that there was nothing such as the Salvation Army, which sometimes passed my home on Sunday. I realized then that it was coming from Heaven. This happened in 1921. We did not have a radio or even a Gramophone.

Mrs. Haines has also stated having heard the NAD during a period of depression over her cat's illness.

On subsequent inquiry, Mrs. Haines informed me that, while she definitely "heard" the music, it did seem to envelop her. The experience, which lasted five minutes, was intuitively thought to be of a religious nature.

Case No. 25 — Peggy Mason

In the last chapter it was mentioned that OOBE cases (including those with NAD) were experienced at childbirth. The case from Mrs. Mason (Sussex, England, in litt., November 11, 1968) is quite similar:

> Owing to my age and a badly broken pelvis earlier in life, I had a Caesarian, but as I wanted to be fully conscious at the birth, this was performed with only a local anesthetic.
> The operation commenced at 9 a.m. on November 18, 1957. Half an hour later my surgeon lifted out the baby,

the cord still unsevered, held it up in both hands like an offering, and said the magic words: "Your baby is born."

Immediately as these words were spoken, I heard a great burst of what I can only call "celestial music." It resounded in my ears—as a sudden unexpected Te Deum with full choir and organ would sound, crashing out in a hitherto silent church. It seemed like a burst of joy, lasting for a few seconds, *then fading away*. I was astonished and quite overcome with the emotion of this unforgettable moment of my life.

This was not the last of the astral music, however. During the week that followed, when my son was brought for me to feed, I enjoyed on several occasions the sound of the most delightful and harmonious singing and music. My small son also heard this, and would turn his head up to gaze to *the ceiling* with rapt attention, as if fascinated by the beautiful sound.

One day I said to the nurse, "Where does that lovely music and singing come from? *It seems to come from the room above.*"

She looked at me curiously and replied, "But there is no room above. I have never heard any music, from anywhere."

Case No. 26 — Mrs. L. C.

Mr. R. C. of London, England (who wishes to remain anonymous), had sent me a note (November 9, 1968) stating that his sister had frequently reported hearing choral and organ music. He quoted her as saying that some of the music was recognized hymns (this phenomenon is quite common with cases related to death), but on other occasions the music was unrecognizable.

In answer to a letter sent to Mr. R. C. and his sister, the following points were brought out—that the music, while "heard," appeared to Mrs. L. C. as subjective, but did not have religious connotations. She further remarked that she has heard choral and organ music simultaneously, which would parallel Mrs. Mason's experience previously quoted.

44

Mr. R. C. also reports some cases, reported to him by his sister, which were related to death. These will be cited in a subsequent chapter.

Case No. 27 — Catherine Mitchell

We have classified OOBEs in two categories: enforced and natural. One form of enforced projection is that caused by anesthetics. Several of these have apparently been caused by ether, chloroform, or nitrous oxide. Several took place during dental operations (for example, Crookall's cases Nos. 358, 362, 363, 365). The following case (*in litt.*, November 8, 1968) was experienced in these exact circumstances:

> I was having teeth out by a dentist in London and was under gas. *I heard the most wonderful orchestral music such as I have never heard before or since.* There was no earthly music being played or relayed there. When I came out of the gas and told the dentist of the marvelous music I had heard, he jokingly said that he would have to charge me extra for that.

Mrs. Mitchell also wrote that she "had neither interest nor knowledge of psychic things" at the time of the experience. Mrs. Mitchell did not feel the experience to be a religious one.

Case No. 28 — Harold Dedman

This case, also heard as a child, was sent to the author by Mr. Dedman (Herts, Great Britain) on November 12, 1968:

> When I was approximately seven or eight years of age, around the years 1922-23, I was occasionally left alone in the house, apart from baby sisters and a brother three years my junior, while my parents visited friends to play cards. Frequently on these occasions I would hear a wonderful choir, composed, I thought, of mostly female voices. I could

never recognize any of the songs or hymns being sung. I was never frightened of this music but looked forward to hearing it. I remember I was curious as to the source of it, as this was before the innovation of radio and none of the adjoining houses had a Gramophone or phonograph.

Sometimes this beautiful singing seemed to fill the room but never did it wake the younger children.

In response to my return letter, Mr. Dedman related that the music which seemed to envelop him usually occurred during the evenings and lasted for five to ten minutes. He also reported having an out-of-the-body experience.

Case No. 29 — E. Thelmar

Miss Thelmar's experience is, like so many cases of NAD, apparently related to the OOBE. This case occurred soon after Miss Thelmar had experimented with astral projection, and could very well have been a side effect of it. The case appears in her book *The Maniac* (Rebman & Co., 1909):

> I began eating, but no sooner had I commenced than I heard a burst of music. It sounded as if massed bands were playing, out of doors, close to the open window.
>
> I stopped eating and listened, entranced. After a few minutes the music suddenly ceased. I recommenced my breakfast. Again another burst of music occurred. I got up and looked out of the window in every direction, to see whence the music proceeded; but there was no band in sight, and apparently no place where any band could possibly be stationed, playing.
>
> Again and again these short outbursts of music occurred.

Miss Thelmar thought the "band" could have been playing Wagner. Her landlady heard nothing.

Case No. 30 — An Elderly Guest

The following case was related in *Light* (April 26, 1884) in which the percipient appears to be in a perfectly normal state. As with other cases previously recounted (for example, Raymond Bayless), the experience was subjective, as no one else heard (or admitted having heard) the music.

The writer of the letter to *Light* states that at her invitation a poor, elderly woman was invited to a tea party. However, instead of waiting for a concert which was to highlight the affair, she abruptly left. Questioned on the following day as to why she hadn't stayed, she replied that people kept talking to her when she was trying to listen.

> Oh my dear lady, it was lovely and I never heard such beautiful music in all my life. [She was then told that no music had been played before she left.] . . . I heard the concert, the whole band. *It began so gently, as a far off music, and they all came swelling in together,* and it was the most heavenly music . . . it was not earthly music; but I heard what I shall never forget and if I shall hear such music in heaven, I am willing to be there now.

Since there was no apparent source to account for her experience, it must be concluded that the music was supraphysical. Note the ever-present crescendo effect.

From these several cases, a few distinct patterns are available for study; though, because of the lack of case histories, these remarks can be only initial and subject to much revision upon further study. Of these seventeen cases (including Case No. 1, which was quoted in the Introduction), we can designate twelve as natural cases, two as enforced, and three that fall into no clear category. While both enforced cases (Nos. 15, 27) heard NAD as orchestral or instrumental, eleven of the twelve natural cases noted hearing the music wholly or in part as choral. As with OOBE cases, natural instances tend toward choral music.

47

Certain natural cases, such as those recounted by Miss Grace Russell, clearly have perceived the music as instrumental. Why? Any artificial catalyst would necessarily deaden the vividness of the experience. (This is more clear in analyzing cases of astral projection. Notice also the way in which enforced OOBEs affected the simultaneous aural phenomena recounted in Chapter 2.) Thus it would appear that natural cases would represent a more perfect form of the phenomenon. A natural complement to this observation would be that hearing NAD as "choral" would be the more developed form of the experience. Hearing "instrumental music" would be a lesser form of the phenomenon. We can now recall that natural projections are more perfect than enforced ones and have greater vividness of experiential awareness. Having classified OOBEs into two categories, we may approach them, as we shall do later with the NAD, as being categorized as those experiences of "nonmediumistic" persons and "mediumistic" persons. The problem to be resolved is whether those cases reported by mediumistic individuals have an experimental content closer to that of natural or enforced cases.

Robert Crookall has outlined the differences between mediumistic and nonmediumistic persons on pages 1 and 43 of *Intimations of Immortality*. Of nonmediumistic persons (ostensibly of natural cases) the experimental content includes:

1. The "double" maintains complete "other-worldness" and cannot manipulate physical matter (for example, telekinetic effects).

2. The ability to have projections is related to the spiritual development of the individual.

3. The "cord" is seen usually connected to the head of the physical body.

4. Perception is clear; no "fog" or "mist" clouds the "double's" vision.

In comparing these four points with mediumistic persons, we find several differences:

1. The "doubles" can influence physical matter.

2. No dependence upon moral scruples is prerequisite for the experience.

3. The "cord" may be attached to the solar plexus.

4. The "double" may view itself as enveloped by "mist."

From a comparison of these two sets of data, obviously mediumistic cases are related to "enforced" cases: Two notable comments amongst the latter are (1) perceiving the "cord" extension via the solar plexus and (2) being enveloped by "mist."

There is here an indication of what we might term a "density factor" that both mediumistic and enforced projections favor. The doctrine of such a "density factor" is ancient, and Crookall gives it the name "vehicle of vitality," which is derived from Hindu terminology. In brief, there appears to be a cohesion which acts as the adhesive between the astral and physical bodies; this cohesive force serves as a "shell" and it is our "density factor." If the astral body is "simple"—for example, during natural cases—this "vehicle of vitality" has remained with the physical body. If the experience is enforced, the astral body is "composite," consisting of both the astral body and etheric shell. This causes, among other things, the observation of being enveloped by mist. It also explains the differences observed during projection in the separate categories. Physical mediums have what Crookall calls a "loose" vehicle of vitality; this then is what creates physical phenomena—an exteriorization of the vehicle of vitality which creates "raps," telekinesis, and the like.

All this seemingly unrelated material has produced a long line of logic which we can now direct toward the NAD. As has been stated several times, both psychic music and the OOBE are "otherworld" experiences and are thus governed by similar directives. Applying Robert Crookall's methods to NAD, we come up with the following systematic statements:

1. Choral music is basically a natural form of the phenomenon and relates to nonmediumistic subjects.

2. Nonvocal music is a product of enforced and mediumistic perceptions. Thus, it is concluded that persons who have apparently

49

natural cases in which orchestral music was heard are in fact mediumistic.

In quoting Miss Russell's case, we have this very situation. From the extract of the correspondence which was incorporated into this chapter, the reader would have no way of knowing that Miss Russell is a mediumistic subject—a designation quite apparent from the many psychic occurrences related by her to me in correspondence.

Another fact is also similar between natural and enforced cases of both the OOBE and NAD. Persons having natural OOBEs are more prone to relate several concordant statements about the sensations of leaving and reentering the physical organism than enforced cases in which, more often than not, the subject becomes conscious after exteriorization.[3]

Rereading the cases in this chapter and the preceding one, it would seem that persons having natural perceptions of psychic music hear it "swell" and decrescendo, while enforced cases (such as Mrs. Mason) more often hear it as a sudden burst—or just simply become aware of it.

In those cases where the subject awoke to hear bursts of music, it would seem, as with several OOBE accounts, that the consciousness gained awareness only after the phenomenon was in progress.

As was my thesis, pointed out at the onset, most of these cases occurred in conditions in which OOBEs also take place. Inasmuch as there are but few differences in the laws governing these two phenomena, we have valid reason to suspect that the NAD is in fact a by-product, or phase, of astral projection.

---

[3] It is not by accident that, during the early history of Western music, only choral music was considered as religious or an art form. Instrumental music was considered degenerate and not proper for liturgical use. (Grout, Donald J.: *History of Western Music* (W. W. Norton & Co., 1960).

Chapter 4

NAD — Related to Death

There is a form of transcendental music which should be of ultimate concern to other parapsychologists, as it was to Ernesto Bozzano—cases related to death.

As a first point, several of the cases to be cited were collectively perceived: That is, more than one individual heard the NAD under such conditions as to make the theory of telepathic transmission among the percipients untenable. This also makes any thought of hallucination invalid, as well as uncovering a causal relation between two events—one we can designate as "psychic," the other death, a phenomenon in itself which has been shown to have a relationship to practically every form of psychical occurrence.

Among spontaneous phenomena alone—apparitions, spontaneous telepathy, spontaneous telekinesis, precognitive dreams—all seem to focus on the moment of death. Thus, apparitions have been seen representing persons who have died at the moment that the apparition was seen, both spontaneous telepathy and precognitive dreams focus on the occurrence of death, and slight telekinetic activity has also been known to precipitate at the point of death (for example, the stopping of clocks and falling of pictures, which may be shown to have a causal nexus with a death).

51

NAD—as a spontaneous phenomenon—is subject both to the wide diversity of forms and theoretical problems to which all spontaneous phenomena are prone. As for forms, we can designate several different ways in which the phenomenon has been recorded:

1. Witnesses at deathbeds have heard "transcendental music."
2. The dying have heard such music, though often it is not heard by others at the deathbed.
3. There have been objective (collective) cases heard in relation to death (in a manner similar to telekinesis related to death).
4. There have been obviously telepathic cases corresponding in time to a death and sometimes associated with death by the percipient.
5. Precognitive cases have been recorded wherein psychic music has served as a premonition of death.

As will be seen, many of the cases herein recounted show regularities within their experimental content which serve not only to concur with experiences observed with NAD heard in OOBEs and normal states, but serve as interconcordance to verify the validity of most of the cases presented.

Music cases related to death were not only of interest to psychists such as Ernesto Bozzano and now, fifty years later, to me but also to the founders of psychical research in Great Britain, who in their monumental collection of spontaneous cases, *Phantasms of the Living*,[1] have categorized a few cases in which music was an active ingredient. Several of these cases show the difficulty in classifying the phenomena as objective or subjective.

Case No. 31 — Mrs. Sewell's Daughter

The important section of this case (Volume II, page 221) refers to the events leading up to the death of Mrs. Sewell's child. "Sounds like the music of an Aeolian harp" were heard, apparently from a cupboard in the room. The swelling effect was also noted: "The sounds increased until the room was full of melody, when it seemed

---

[1] Gurney, Podmore, and Myers (Kegan Paul, 1886).

slowly to pass down the stairs and ceased. The servants in the kitchen, two stories below, heard the sounds." The phenomenon became recurrent and, though collectively perceived, was not heard by the girl herself. The music was also heard when the little girl died.

Case No. 32 — Mrs. L.

This case, recounted in *Phantasms of the Living* (page 446), was heard after the death of Mrs. L. by three persons designated as Eliza W., Charlotte, and Doctor G. It manifested as a group of women's voices singing softly like the sounds of an *Aeolian harp* (note similarity to preceding case). Another person present, Mr. L., did not hear anything unusual. Eliza W. heard the words, "The strife is o'er, the battle done," while the two others heard the music differently.

Case No. 33 — Miss Yates's Daughter

A third *Phantasms* case (Volume II, page 223) records Mrs. Yates hearing, after her daughter's death at the age of twenty-one, music "such as mortals never sing."

This early collection, first appearing in 1886, has further instances of celestial music, but these will be put into the context of the chapter.

Case Type I — Music Heard at Deathbeds

Case No. 34 — Mrs. A. C. F.

The short experience written by Mrs. A. C. F. (Hants, Great Britain) was printed in the *Psychic News*, August 6, 1966:

> My brother was lying desperately ill in a North London hospital last year. His wife, my other brother, and I stayed all night in the waiting room expecting an urgent summons to the ward at any moment.

My sister-in-law slept on the bed completely exhausted. My brother and I sat whispering to one another through the night.

At about 3:14 a.m. a single bird started to chirp in the darkness outside the window. We both left our chairs and went to look out. We could see nothing.

As we walked to our chairs, the room was suddenly *filled with the sound of an organ playing and voices singing a hymn* [note the similarity of this combination to cases quoted in the last chapter]. I remarked on the loudness of the "nurses' services" at such an hour in the morning. It was not until several hours later that I realized that the chapel where we had prayed in the day had only a piano and no organ.

My brother passed on the next day. I believe I had an impression from the Spirit World and that the voices I heard belonged to those on the other side who also loved him and who had come to help him make the transition.

Mrs. A. C. F. has offered me several details (in litt. November 12, 1968) worthy of attention. For one, she states, "I have since contacted the matron at the hospital and she assures me the nurses never hold services in the Chapel there." While she notes that her brother heard nothing, she wrote that "the music was so powerful it vibrated through the floor and up through the walls of the large waiting room and *gradually faded out.*"

Case No. 35 — H. D. Jencken

This case reported by H. D. Jencken is one of the oldest on record within the span of organized research, and was given as testimony for the *Report on Spiritualism of the Committee of the London Dialectical Society,* 1873. The brief case merely states, "At the passing away of an old servant of our household, a strain of solemn music, at about four in the morning, was, by the nurse and servants, heard in the room of the dying woman; the music lasting fully twenty minutes."

Case Type II — Observations of the Dying

Case No. 36 — A Pious Man

One of the oldest cases of this type may be found in the *Dialogues of St. Gregory* (edited by E. Gardner, London, 1911, page 195), who in speaking of a particularly pious man states, "while he lay giving ear within himself to that divine harmony, his holy soul departed this mortal life."

Case No. 37 — Peter Nielsen

A somewhat more complete account comes to us from Margaret Focht (Horsham, Pennsylvania) and was recently published in *Fate Magazine* (October, 1968):

> My mother, Frida Lustrap, has told me many times that when her father, Peter Emil Nielsen, died in the winter of 1914 she and my grandmother Rosmine knew he saw something extraordinary.
> Peter Nielsen was fifty-three when he died of stomach cancer. In the terminal stages he was at home in Aarhus, Denmark, and for three months had eaten almost nothing. He was emaciated and too weak to move. No word had he spoken in that time, and even his comprehension seemed to disappear. He was just a shell.
> The doctors had said his death was near, so my mother and grandmother took turns keeping constant vigil. For some reason, however, both of them were at his deathbed when the end came.
> Suddenly grandfather, who had been barely breathing, sat upright in bed. Before either of the women could rush to ease him back, his eyes opened wide and he exclaimed loudly, and joyfully, "The angels are singing! How beautiful it is." There was a long pause and then he said, "And I'm coming too!" He looked excited and happy as he spoke. Then just as suddenly, quite calmly and peacefully, he lay back on the pillow and died."

Case No. 38 — Colonel . . . . . .

This lengthy account is taken from the annals of the Society for Psychical Research and was published in their *Proceedings,* Vol. III, page 92:

Some sixteen years since, Mrs.....................said to me, "We have some people staying here all next week. Do you know any person I could get to sing with the girls?" I suggested that my gunmaker, Mr. X., had a daughter with a fine voice, who was training as a public singer, and that I would write to X. and ask if he would allow her to come down and spend a week with us. On my wife's approval I wrote and Miss X. came down for a week, and then left. As far as I know Mrs............. never saw her again. Shortly after, I called on X., thanked him for allowing his daughter to come to us, and said we were all much pleased with her. X. replied: "I fear you have spoilt her, for she says she never passed so happy a week in her life." Miss X. did not come out as a singer, but shortly after married Mr. Z. and none of us ever saw her again.

Six or seven years passed and Mrs. ...., who had been long ill, was dying, in fact she did die the following day. I was sitting at the foot of her bed talking over some business matters that she was anxious to arrange, being perfectly composed and in thorough possession of her senses. She changed the subject and said, "Do you hear those voices singing?" I replied that I did not, and she said, "I have heard them several times today and I am sure they are the angels welcoming me to Heaven"; but, she added, "It is strange, there is one voice amongst them I am sure I know, and I cannot remember whose voice it is." Suddenly she stopped and said, pointing straight over my head, "Why, there she is in the corner of the room; it is Julia X.; she is coming on; she is leaning over you; she has her hands up, she is praying; do look, she is going." I turned but could see nothing. Mrs. .... then said, "She is gone." All these things I imagined to be the phantasies of a dying person.

Two days afterward, taking up the *Times* newspaper, I saw recorded the death of Julia Z., wife of Mr. Z. I was so astounded that in a day or so after the funeral I asked Mr. X. if Mrs. Z., his daughter, was dead. He said, "Yes, poor thing, she died of puerperal fever. On the day she died she began singing in the morning, and sang and sang until she died." Colonel .... adds later:

Mrs. Z. died on February 2nd at six or thereabout in the morning, 1874. Mrs. .... died, February 13, 1874, at about four in the evening. I saw notice of Mrs. Z.'s death of February 14th. Mrs. .... never was subject to hallucinations of any sort.

Case Type III — Objective Cases Related to Death

Case No. 39 — E. I.

This case (*Phantasms*, Volume II, page 639) was originally written as a diary entry and was not composed with the thought of being published—being so, it is most evidential since, aside from the honesty of the facts, there is little logical reason for the case to have been written out.

Just after Mrs. L.'s death, between two and three a.m., I heard a most sweet and singular strain of singing outside the windows. It died after passing the house. All in the room heard it, and the medical attendant, who was still with us, went to the window as I did and looked out, but there was nobody there. It was a bright and beautiful night. *It was as if several voices were singing in perfect unison a sweet melody which died away in the distance.* Two persons had gone from the room to fetch something and were coming back upstairs at the back of the house, and heard singing and stopped, saying, "What is that singing?" They could not naturally have heard any sound outside the windows in the front of the house from where they were. I cannot think that any explanation can be given to this—as I think—supernatural singing, but it would be very interesting to me to know what is said by those who have made such matters a subject of study.

F. W. H. Myers, who was one of the founding members of the Society for Psychical Research and who quotes this narrative in his *Human Personality and Its Survival of Bodily Death*, made some highly interesting comments about the case. First, he linked phantasmal music with apparitions and felt that instances such as these "may be as clear a manifestation of personality as phantasmal figures." Clearly Myers went into the realms of implicating survival of death which Bozzano would reevaluate years later. Secondly Myers noted that hearing actual music is rarer than singing. This hits upon an important point—we have already classified "singing" as an experience of natural OOBEs and "orchestral" music as a product of enforced OOBEs. Myers had thus, when his volume was posthumously published in 1903, made an observation which has been quite independently corroborated by us today—that more natural cases of the phenomenon seem to be reported than enforced cases. Of Robert Crookall's material, about two hundred and fifty natural OOBEs are listed, in contrast to only about fifty enforced ones. So it is both natural and significant that Myers notes that instrumental music is rarer than singing with this "other-world" experience.

Also, Myers is speaking, it would seem, of music phenomena occurring at the point of death, which is a "natural" projection hardly ever having the properties of "enforced" projection.

Case No. 40 — H. E. L.

Myers writes (*Human Personality and Its Survival of Bodily Death*, abridgement, University Books, 1961):

A gentleman named H. E. L., who is a master at Eton College, wrote to us telling about the beautiful music heard by people in the house just about ten minutes after his mother died. He did not hear it himself. He endorsed two memorandums written by witnesses.

Case No. 41 — Mrs. Horne

This old case (*Journal* S. P. R., Volume VI, page 27) graphically illustrates Myers's contention that this music may be connected to the personality of the individuals concerned (as was seen in Case 38). The case is recounted by the percipient's daughter:

It is nearly thirty years now, but it is as vividly impressed upon her memory. She was sitting in the dining room (in a self-contained chair) which was behind the drawing room, with Jamie my eldest brother, on her knee, who was then a baby scarcely two years old. The nurse had gone out for the afternoon, and there was no one in the house except the maid downstairs. The doors of the dining room and drawing room both happened to be open at the time. All at once she heard the most divine music, very sad and sweet, which lasted for about two minutes, then *gradually died away*. My brother jumped from my mother's knee, exclaiming, "Papa, Papa," and ran through the drawing room.

Mama felt as if she could not move and rang the bell for a servant, whom she told to go and see who was in the drawing room. When she went into the room, she found my brother standing beside the piano saying, "No papa." Why the child should have exclaimed these words was that papa was very musical and used often to go straight to the piano when he came home. [This implies that the psychic music was keyboard, though this is not clearly stated.] Such was the impression on mama that she noted the time to a minute, and six weeks after, she received a letter saying that her sister had died at the Cape, and the time corresponded exactly to the minute that she had heard the music. I may tell you that my aunt was a very fine musician.

Case No. 42 — Sarah Jenkins

An extremely lengthy case, collectively perceived, was published in the *Journal* S. P. R., February, 1893, and was from an American correspondent. While most music cases are described by their percipients as "choral" or "singing," this one, like several others, attempts no description—no reference to any musical genre is made. The music also *died away*, which is quite common. In strong contrast is that the music was heard as a strong burst, which is inconsistent with most narratives; however, it is reported in enforced cases. This example may serve, then, as an anomaly; it too was related to a musically gifted individual and is quoted in full from the original source:

In the year 1845 Mr. Herwig, a German and a much-esteemed musician, who had for several years resided in Boston, Massachusetts, died suddenly in that city. I was then a young girl, and knew him only through his high reputation, and my own great enjoyment of his delightful performances on the violin in public concerts. The only personal association I ever had with him was that in the winter before his death, in returning to my home from that of a friend who was studying with me, I chanced for many weeks to meet Mr. Herwig almost daily on a certain part of Beacon Street. It seemed to be only an accident, but finally it became such a constant occurrence that he smiled on me kindly, and gave me a respectful little bow, which I ventured as respectfully to return.

The following autumn he died, as I have said, very suddenly, and his funeral took place on November 4, 1845, in Trinity Church—then on Summer Street, Boston. It was a solemn and touching service, attended by a crowd of musicians and other eminent citizens; for all mourned the loss of such an accomplished and valuable man. I was present with my sister, and, in the midst of the services, there came to me a most unaccountable and inexpressible feeling that he might then and there at once rise from the coffin and appear in life again among us. Hardly knowing what I did, I caught my sister's hand, exclaiming almost aloud, "Oh, he must, he must come to life again!" so very earnestly that she looked at me in wonder and whispered "Hush! Hush!" That evening my mother, my two sisters, a friend (Mr. S., from Cuba), and myself—five of us in all—were sitting in our dining room, No. 4, H. Street, Boston, while my sister and I were describing the funeral. My sister had just told of my singular exclamation while there, and I was repeating the words, when suddenly the room was filled with a burst of glorious music, such as none of us had ever heard. I saw a look of astonishment and even fear on every face, and, in a sort of fright myself, I continued speaking incoherently when, once more, after a slight pause, *came a similar swell of harmony which then died softly away.* My sister and I at once rushed to the hall door, which was but a few steps from us, to discover if outside there were any music, but we heard not a sound save the hard drizzle of a dark rainy night. I then ran upstairs to the parlour over the dining room, where was only a Quaker lady reading. A piano was in that room and, though it was closed, I asked, "Has anyone been playing?" "No," she replied, "but I heard a strange burst of music. What was it?"

Now, let it be understood that, as a family, we had never been superstitious, but on the contrary had been educated to scoff at the idea of ghosts, omens, etc., so that none of us announced this occurrence as supernatural, but could only look at each other saying, "What was it?" The Quakeress, however, we found more excited than ourselves. She related the experience to her daughters, who were absent at the time, and they spent much time in perambulating the neighborhood to discover if there had been any music in the houses near ours; but it was distinctly proved that there had been none, nor had any been heard from the street. In fact, what we heard seemed to be close around ourselves, as we each described it, and unlike any we had ever heard.

It may seem strange that, after so many years, I should be able to describe so particularly this event. But I own it made a deep impression upon the minds of all the hearers. I have often narrated it, and heard the others narrate it in exactly the same way, and my sister, the only one now living of that little company, will verify my description word for word.

61

I add my replies to some questions which have been asked.

When we went to the hall door, we looked up and down the street, which was well lighted. Street performers upon musical instruments were absolutely unknown in Boston at this period.

Mrs. S., the Quaker lady of whom I have spoken, was staying in the house as a guest. I asked whether anyone had played upon the piano, not because the music bore any resemblance to that of a piano, but to connect it, if possible, with some natural cause.

The music appeared to all of us to be in the room where we were sitting. It seemed to begin in one corner, and to pass round the room. I said that it was like a burst of sunshine in sound and can give no better description of it.

My mother and Mrs. S. agreed that the music was utterly inexplicable.

My sister and I, as well as the daughters of Mrs. S., made thorough inquiries at all the houses about us, but could hear nothing that could account for the phenomenon.

Miss E. Jenkins corroborated her sister's account and testified to its accuracy.

Case No. 43 — Salvation Army Worker

Again we shall turn to rather old reports. This account is not taken from psychic literature but appeared as a newspaper story (*Daily Chronicle*, Great Britain, May 4, 1905), which shows that the phenomenon is not imprisoned within "borderline" journals. The woman involved was a Salvation Army worker:

> For three or four nights mysterious and sweet music was heard in her bedroom at frequent intervals by relatives and friends, lasting on each occasion about a quarter of an hour. *At times the music appeared to be from a distance, and then would gradually grow in strength* while the young woman lay unconscious.

Case No. 44 — William Stephens

Our final example in this category is found in as unlikely a place as W. T. Stead's magazine-paper *More Ghost Stories* (special Christmas and New Year's edition), which comprised accounts sent to its author *in litt*:

> My grandfather on my mother's side, William Stephens, lived in Bridgeport, in Dorsetshire. His eldest son, also named William Stephens, lived on the Island of Guernsey. One night he and his wife were awakened by strains of exquisitely beautiful music, more beautiful, they say, than any they had ever heard before. Shortly afterward they heard that my grandfather had died that same night and, as they afterward found, at the same hour that they awoke from their sleep.

Before moving on to the next set of case studies, which fall into a category slightly unrelated to the three I have already presented, some pertinent comments should be offered. Again, this discussion is related to the NAD and the OOBE.

Of those cases which were recorded by deathbed visitants, certain cases (Mrs. A. C. F., Mrs. L., Mrs. Yates) recorded the phenomenon as choral. It has been said, in connection with another case, that the death experience is in fact the same as the OOBE: Persons have the experience near death, and several mediumistic "communications" describe the death experience as being the same as the OOBE; further, several projectors have changed environment[2] and have recorded meeting the "dead." These were *natural* projections (near or at the point of death) and correspond with NAD being heard at or near the point of death in *natural* states—choral.

This is more clearly seen in our cases wherein the dying themselves heard the music—always as choral. Some highly concordant points now present themselves as to the source of the music. Both Peter Nielsen (Case No. 37) and Mrs. .... (Case No. 38) felt the

---

[2] See Chapter 2.

music to be emanating from "discarnates." While Mr. Nielsen's comments were intuitive, Mrs. .... heard a recognized voice and saw an apparition of that person near the time of her death. This is in full agreement with some OOBEs, such as that of J. W. Skelton, who saw "angels singing" (Case No. 13). We have here an important point—that the dying attribute the NAD to discarnates.

It has been shown several times that (accepting survival after death) discarnates help during the death experience. Karlis Osis has shown in his important monograph *Death-bed Observations by Physicians and Nurses* that the dying recognize relatives or friends greeting them. Even Charles Richet (*Thirty Years of Psychical Research*, Macmillan, 1923), who was an anti-survivalist, gave attention to this phenomenon, especially in those cases where the dying see discarnate friends of whom they have had no knowledge of their death; and considered them as strong evidence in favor of survival. Dr. Osis also seems to favor the survival explanation. Crookall has analyzed the experience in *The Supreme Adventure* (see Appendices). The phenomenon is set beyond telepathically induced hallucination in those few cases where apparitional forms have become collectively perceived by deathbed observers.

Having resolved that discarnates are in some way involved in the death experience, and may also accompany the hearing of transcendental music, it is up to us to complete the pattern by showing that discarnates are also active during the OOBE.

Both spiritualist belief and some good empirical data suggest that the "dead" come to help the newly dead by aiding them in their release from the physical body. The same is true with the OOBE. Of two hundred and fourteen "natural cases" of projection analyzed by Crookall, 22 percent note seeing discarnates.[3] Several of the

---

[3] Case Nos. 1, 2, 4, 8, 11, 13, 24, 27, 30, 34, 48, 49, 62, 63, 64, 66, 69, 70, 74, 76, 81, 92, 98, 99, 113, 181, 184, 208, 215, 216, 218, 223, 225, 230, 234, 247, 248, 251, 264, 288, 289, 293, 295, 296, 300, 302, 307, 313, 319, 332, 333. Of the "enforced type," Nos. 132, 140, 352, 367, 368, 382. (Crookall: *The Study and Practice of Astral Projection* and *More Astral Projections*.) Also see p. 144, *More Astral Projections*.

accounts note that these "dead" serve as "helpers" who aid in the exteriorization of the double. This is similar to what is described at the death experience. Mr. J. A. Lilley (Crookall, Case No. 184) felt discarnate hands lift his body out of its physical shell. This is fairly typical.

Some of our reports (such as Mrs. Henley's) saw both "helpers" and heard music. From this we can summarize a long list of logical coefficients:

1. That music is heard by both the dying and the projected.
2. That dying and the OOBE are virtually the same thing.
3. Discarnates aid in both dying and projecting.
4. The dying have both heard music and seen the "dead."
5. Thus a causal relationship seems to exist between the NAD and the activities of the "dead."

Our explanation for all these interrelationships may seem quite naïve, but nevertheless it fits the facts neatly. At the point of death and during the OOBE, the hypothetical "psychic ether" which separates mind and matter, and borders the physical and the post-mortem world, becomes quite fine. That unknown substance which serves as a boundary between worlds is "softened." Is it then any wonder that so many psychical phenomena seem to focus about death? Thus any properties of the "other-world" become momentarily revealed to the living. Therefore it is not surprising that not only the dying should hear music, but also the living gathered around their deathbeds. But what of cases related to death and heard at a distance? We now penetrate into quite another matter—the relationship between NAD, OOBEs, and apparitions.

When the early Society for Psychical Research founders began to study spontaneous case material, they discovered that a strong percentage of the histories they had received noted seeing apparitions closely related to the time of the agent's death. These reports were published as the *Census of Hallucination* (1894) and noted two apparition "types"—those of the dead and those of the living (ostensible astral projections). The relationship between these two apparitional types was not to be made clear until 1956 when Professor Hornell Hart and his collaborators published their *Six Theories about Apparitions*, a cooperative report by the International Project for Research in ESP Projection (*Proceedings* S.P.R., Volume 50). In this study Hart shows that apparitions of the dead have no substantially different characteristics from those of the living. So we find that apparitions of the dead *are* in fact of the same nature as apparitions of the living. (A summary of this work may be found in the *International Journal of Parapsychology*, March, 1967.)

From a theoretical standpoint we must find an explanation which will cover both genres equally well. Hart rejected the theory that apparitions were, in fact, "doubles," as he felt it could not cover certain facts such as the "clothing" of apparitions. He favored the "etheric-object" of Raynor Johnson, which does view the apparition as objective and a phenomenon indicative of survival. Physical theories of apparitions have been expounded as far back as F. W. H. Myers. This theory need not be discussed in detail, though it states that apparitions may work within the framework of the physical and mental. In other words, it is not "subjective" but "supraphysical" and works via "the psychic ether"—that borderline state between mind and matter—and would be contingent upon the perceptions of both.

However, Hart's laudable study was composed before Crookall's work was available for study. Crookall's carefully detailed and comprehensive works supply us with material which allows us to accept that apparitions *are* structured by the "double." At death the double retains the whole of the vehicle of vitality (the density factor), which is actually ideoplastic in nature and, being variable as well as dense, could easily model itself into the replica of clothing. All this is explained in his *The Next World—and the Next*. (See Appendices.) It may still be said that some apparitions are the product of telepathic hallucination—and there is no reason to reject the idea that any phenomenon may have more than one means of production—but the cases wherein apparitions are collectively seen or influence material objects (telekinesis) must have some physical properties delegated to them.

All this discussion finally brings us back to the NAD heard at a distance at the time of the agent's death. If the agent can project his "other-world" body to the percipient, is it not possible that either (1) he may inadvertently send other experiences of the death experience also, or (2) in transferring his consciousness (and apparitions show every property of having intent and consciousness) could not the weakness in the psychic ether also be transferred and perceived even though the other-world body remains invisible?

To summarize—the death experience causes a weakness in the "psychic ether." Transferring the "other-world" body to a distant place (an incipient apparition) also transfers the weakness in the ether, which may be more perceivable to the percipients than the "other-world" body itself. Thus, any properties of the "other world" such as celestial music may become perceivable and so, also, related to a coincidental death.

This may serve as our explanation for these cases. As for NAD and the OOBE, the theory is self-explanatory—again a weakness in the psychic ether which causes the projectors to hear music. Since the OOBE and NAD occur generally in the same conditions, it is clear that those conditions which are inducive to the OOBE also cause weakness in the ether. Thus the NAD may be heard (sometimes objectively and sometimes subjectively) in ostensibly normal states when the weakness has been produced and the person involved has not yet realized that an incipient OOBE is taking place; or because of certain properties within the double (for example, a particularly dense "vehicle of vitality") an OOBE cannot take place.

We have seen various interconnections between the OOBE, death, psychic music, and apparitions. A suitable theory must be found to explain them, and the one presented here seems to fill this need fully.

We end with a case including all of these phenomena, quoted from James H. Hyslop's *Contact with the Other World* (The Century Co., 1919):

67

Case No. 45 — A. B. Weymouth

When I was living in Los Angeles, California, I became acquainted with Mrs. Jennie D., who seemed to be a congenial soul. In the autumn of 1888, Mrs. D. and I made a verbal agreement that the one who should first enter the spiritual world should return (d.v.) and appear to the other. In the spring of 1898, the lady became seriously ill and after a few months of suffering passed away. As no tidings came from the deceased, I supposed that some unexpected obstacle prevented her return. But at last the long silence was broken. On Saturday evening, October 22, 1910, I retired to rest soon after nine o'clock. After refreshing sleep I awoke, with the impression that something unusual was about to happen. Then I distinctly heard a voice saying: "Jennie D. is coming." A few moments later, something like a bright cloud appeared in my bedroom. In the midst of the cloud I recognized the form of my long lost friend. While hovering in the air, she sang two verses sweetly. Then other spirit forms appeared (the faces not recognized) and joined in the refrain. I had never heard the words or the music before; and I regret that I cannot recall the words. They were very beautiful and so was the melody. When the music ceased, the bright cloud and the celestial visitors disappeared and my room was dark again. I rose immediately, lighted a lamp, looked at my watch and made a record of the incident. The time of the vision was 12:30 on Sunday morning.

Case Types IV and V — Telepathic and Precognitive Cases

A clue to the understanding of the following group of reports is related to our studies of cases in normal states—that there is only a fine line between subjective and objective modes of the phenomenon.

These cases are all what we could term "subjective" (though I should prefer, and have suggested, the term "supraphysical") and, since they fall into actually the same category as other cases related to death, some theoretical relationship must exist between these and the previous examples.

This brings us to the problem of reciprocity. There exists a myth in parapsychology which seeks to define clearly telepathy as proceeding from an agent and received like a radio by a percipient. Thus a graphic view lends itself well to the explanation of telepathy by some sort of brain wave. Unfortunately this theory is shattered when we realize that telepathic impressions do not follow the laws governing "waves"—no attenuation, no clear-cut agent and percipient.

Parapsychologists have tried to revise the view that telepathy is a clearly defined agent-percipient experience. In fact, the modern trend in this field seems to prefer to designate both parties in a telepathic experience as "active." In other words, the agent-percipient view is obsolete. This was Tyrrell's problem in trying to solve the enigma of apparitions: that directives from both sides interplay during the experience.[4]

To fit all these theories in relation to a psychic ether, we no longer have a "discontinuation" (weakness) in the ether, but a "reflection." This is reciprocal between two parties. It also relates telepathic cases to objective ones. Two persons may now share, though by no normal sensory means, common experiences and perceptions. Thus, hearing music may be either a reflection of the experience of a dying person, or the manner in which the subconscious mind (since telepathic impressions work through the subconscious) seeks to depict the events to the consciousness. On reviewing the following few cases, I think the first explanation is more comprehensible. It must be remembered that we are now concerned with a phenomenon which is being projected through the mind and thus would be colored by it, so that obvious patterns such as found with other genres of the phenomenon are no longer decipherable.

---

[4] Tyrrell, G. N. M., 1942, Myers Memorial Lecture.

Case No. 46 — Camille Saint-Saëns

Our first case comes from Camille Saint-Saëns, the famous French composer (1835-1921). In the last chapter of *NAD*, several cases were quoted where the agent was musically oriented. Here we have a case in which the "percipient" was musically talented. This illustrates the close interworking of the agent-percipient relationship. The case is quoted from Camille Flammarion in *Death and Its Mystery* (The Century Co., 1921), Flammarion reported that he received a letter from Saint-Saëns stating that in January, 1871, during the last days of the Franco-Prussian War, he was celebrating with some friends:

> . . . when suddenly I heard in my head a plaintive musical theme, of dolorous chords, which I have since used for the commencement of my *Requiem*, and I felt in my inmost being a presentiment of some misfortune. A profound anxiety unnerved me. That was the moment when Henri Regnault, to whom I was very much attached, was killed.

Case No. 47 — Emma Powell

Mrs. Powell's narrative, like that of her OOBE case, incorporated into Chapter 2, was given to me on tape:

> When I was seventeen I had had a bad sore throat and I was recovering and was sitting up in bed. My mother and father were in the room with me. I heard a quartet singing, "Nearer My God to Thee" and I could hear all the parts —soprano, alto, tenor, and bass—it was very beautiful. I asked them if they could hear it and they said "No" and that I was imagining it. And then this same quartet sang "Church in the Wildness" and it was beautiful. But they couldn't hear that either. Then I heard a man start to speak and they couldn't hear that either. It was very plain to me that it was a funeral speech. So I just got out of bed and that was all of it. But then we heard on Monday that a very dear cousin had passed on.

Cases No. 48-49 — Mr. C., Elizabeth Hyams

Two correspondents have described precognitive cases—that is, music occurring before the actual death took place. Mr. C., who wished to remain anonymous and who was mentioned in a previous chapter, reports that his sister often hears the national anthem of Great Britain before a death in the royal family. Mrs. Elizabeth Hyams writes (November 13, 1968, from Essex, Great Britain) that music "comes only when a dear friend is passing over to the other side, and I hear the news of a sudden passing over in a day or so."

Case No. 50 — M. Revell

This correspondent (London, November 14, 1968) differs in her report in that the music was not described as beautiful at all, but represented a rather distressing experience. Mrs. Revell has reported having several precognitive experiences:

> I had an experience you may be interested in about twenty-one years ago. My sister and I, with two small children, paid a visit home. My father had been ill, but had recovered enough to be up and around. When we retired to bed the evening before returning to our homes, I lay awake for a while and gradually became aware of music in the distance—only it had no melody. It was a haunting, wailing sound and I fell asleep still listening. . . . As soon as I awoke, the wailing musical noise seemed to be everywhere and, as we had to travel to London from Guesborough, Yorkshire, that night by coach, I was sure there was going to be an accident. On enquiring no one else had heard the music and I do not think I mentioned that I was still hearing it, and not until I left the house that night did it cease.
>
> We all arrived safely enough. My father died four months later.

I think this is a case of premonition of death. It does not fit in

71

with persons hearing NAD in normal states. Further Mrs. Revell's description of the music is reminiscent of the lore of the "Banshee Wail." Probably cases such as these (along with apparitions seen by the dying) served to create the legend.

Chapter 5

NAD, Hauntings, and the Psychic Ether

We have seen that one phenomenon—celestial music—has directed us through various channels of psychical investigations: From a relatively "simple" base of one of a few "other-world" experiences, it has implicated other phenomena of the same category. In the process, it has drawn upon apparitional experiences, telepathic experiences, and the activities of the "dead."

All these characteristics of the NAD finally merge into the para-psychologists' *ultimate concern* (to borrow Tillich's phrase), where we can no longer distinguish the objective from the subjective, sense perception from psychic perception, the thought process of the living from that of the "dead," and even the almost total destruction of the ether field separating the two worlds we have postulated. This grandiose enigma is that of hauntings. And yet, within the boundaries of the diverse phenomena associated with haunted houses, our celestial music, which began as an insignificant psychic curio, still gleams through.

The existence of musical phenomena in hauntings has a very basic theoretical bearing: that these data should help explain hauntings and that, inversely, any theory of hauntings should explain these data. This is little more than a matter of logic.

We need not outline what or what not a haunting is. Every reader of any psychic book has some comprehension of what entails a haunting, and it would be laborious to outline once again their characteristics. However, this can not be said of everyone's comprehension of what the involved theoretical mechanics of hauntings encompass.

The following are a few cases of haunting reports where music was heard. Subsequently they will be examined in relation to the five classical theories of hauntings and the revised ones which have been presented in recent years.

Case No. 51 — Abbey of Jumieges

The phantom monks of the Abbey of Jumieges are famous. These phantoms have been seen and heard chanting in medieval fashion by several witnesses. Mrs. Sidgwick wrote briefly of the reports (*Journal* S.P.R., Volume XVIII, page 118): ". . . We have the evidence of four members of a family who, in the ruins of the Abbey of Jumieges, heard for a few seconds sounds as of monks singing. Their efforts to discover any natural cause for this failed, but whether the possibilities were exhausted may perhaps be doubted."

In this same connection there are several classical reports of phantom assemblies of chanting monks, some extremely well witnessed. This one slight instance is fairly representative of them all.

Case No. 52 — Mary Jobson

A haunting-poltergeist case of an earlier era was reported in full in Catherine Crowe's *The Night Side of Nature* (Routledge Co., 1848), in which music was frequently heard. Miss Crowe describes the aural phenomena quite enthusiastically:

> One of the most remarkable features in this case is the beautiful music which was heard by all the parties including the unbelieving father, and, indeed, it seems to have been, in a great degree, that this converted him at last. This music

was heard repeatedly during a space of sixteen weeks; sometimes it was like an organ, but more beautiful, there was singing of holy songs, in parts, and the words being distinctly heard.

Some of the music centered on the illness of Mary Jobson, a twelve-year-old girl, around whom the whole haunting-poltergeist took place. Unlike many instances of music related to death (or illness), the music in this haunting continued after the girl's recovery.

Case No. 53 — Anne H.

A somewhat more traditional haunting was recorded in the S.P.R. *Proceedings*, Volume VI. The location of this British haunting was not revealed. Being of a "traditional" nature, the diversity of phenomena was quite extensive. The testimony we draw from is that of Anne H., a servant of the house's occupant, Mrs. G.

Anne H. notes (recorded June 16, 1888) hearing strange noises, footsteps, screams, mysterious knockings and bell ringings, and movement of objects. Though Anne H. reported seeing none, apparitions were also a part of the manifestations. Of one outbreak of phenomena the servant wrote:

> Then we used to hear a great crash every night about 10 o'clock, it was downstairs in the kitchen. I used to think everything was being smashed; then one night it seemed as if some one was out on the landing slipping about; then we heard some music, it sounded like a musical box to me; it played three times. . . .

Case No. 54 — Brook House

The haunting of Brook House (in Great Britain, actual locality never given) must remain an unsolved mystery. If we are to believe the reports, it must have been the wildest haunting in all psychic annals: apparitions, objects displaced, voices, and so on. Apparently

Edmund Gurney, one of the founding members of the Society for Psychical Research and principal author of *Phantasms of the Living,* was interested in the house but never received any substantial reports. Here we draw from a written account of a Mr. B., who was involved in some of the outbreaks, and which was communicated to Mr. Ralph Hastings, one of the principals in the haunting. He in turn sent the account to W. T. Stead and it was incorporated in *Real Ghost Stories.* The incident is paraphrased by Hastings:

> The sound as of a woman's voice, wailing quietly, but with unbelievable sorrow, came sighing to his ears. He listened acutely, and words unspoken, borne on the drowsy air, seemed to whisper their reflected meaning to his senses. They died away and faint sounds as of "far away" music, most mournful and soul-saddening, appealed to him. They sang or seemed to sing the "Story of the House." *The Aeolian strains rose higher,* as if the long-drawn-out and pent-up agony of years would burst its bonds. *Then, as if constrained by a Master hand, they faltered, sobbed, then ceased.*

Case No. 55 — Hinton Ampner Haunting

The Hinton Ampner case (England) apparently began in 1755, and the last record of any phenomena was almost twenty years later in 1772. The house was destroyed in 1773. Among the phenomena were apparitions and the usual array of ghostly manifestations. The case is recorded in Harry Price's *Poltergeist over England* (London, Country Life, 1945). Mrs. Mary Ricketts recorded in her narrative that, along with hearing voices, groans, and shrieks, some more pleasant sounds were perceived: "Several times I heard sounds of harmony within the room—no distinct or regular notes, but a vibration of harmonious tones."

Case No. 56 — Willington Mill

One of the longer hauntings on record was the complex manifestation in Great Britain's Willington Mill, which spread from 1835 to

1867. Apparitions were seen: knockings, footsteps, whistling, and music. The source is the *Journal* of the S.P.R., Volume V, 1891-92, pages 331-52. The music consisted of bell sounds. The report reads:

> On the 21st, J. and E. P. heard a handbell ring upstairs; they were quite satisfied at the time that no one was there. On the 28th, heavy thumps in the middle of the night, and after breakfast the next morning E. P. heard a handbell rung upstairs when she was quite certain everyone was downstairs. J. and E. P. are sure it is no actual bell in their home that is rung, the tone being altogether different.

Minor musical sounds such as this have been known not only in haunting cases, but with mediums as well. A delicate bell sound was produced by the Boston medium Margery and is discussed in the next chapter.

Case No. 57 — Solmon Haunting

This case was communicated by correspondence to Harry Price and is in his book *Poltergeist over England*. In a letter (January, 1943) to Price, Mrs. Violet L. Solmon wrote: "Once in the garden I heard an organ playing. It was in the summer and I can only describe it as incredibly 'beautiful.'"

Among the other phenomena were apparitions, footsteps, opening and shutting of doors, lights, and similar manifestations.

Case No. 58 — The Bell Witch

The Bell Witch, an American case of the last century, was recorded primarily in W. V. Ingram's *Authenticated History of the Bell Witch* (Rare Book Reprints, 1961). No one can tell the true extent of the case since all our reports are both exaggerated and badly researched. Fraud seems probable for some of the outbreaks, but in general it seems to be one of those common cases where both real and dubious phenomena took place.

Sometimes an invisible choir "would treat our company to some delightful singing, a regular concert of rich feminine voices, modulating to the sweetest cadence and intonation, singing any hymn called for with solemnity and wonderful effect."

Case No. 59 — A Haunted Churchyard

The next example was recorded in Sir Ernest Bennett's *Apparitions and Haunted Houses* (Faber & Faber, Ltd., 1939). The case, almost entirely of music, is self-explanatory and was described in a letter to Bennett dated July 23, 1889.

It affords me much pleasure, in answer to your letter of the 20th which I only received today, to give you an account of my experiences in connection with the music in D. woods, which does not seem due to any ordinary source.

I have heard it, I think, four times, and always at the same place, viz. on the public road which runs along the south bank of the Tweed, and which passes at the distance of three-quarters of a mile the old churchyard of D. The churchyard, from which the music always seems to come, is south of the road, and at a much higher elevation, and the intervening ground is densely covered with wood. The first two or three times I heard the sound it was very faint, but sufficiently distinct to enable me to follow the swellings and cadences. I do not know why, but on those occasions I never for a moment thought it was real music. Neither did I think it anything very unusual, though the tones seemed more ethereal than any I had heard before. I am exceedingly fond of music, and in my walks, frequently sing without sound (if I may use such an expression) tunes, pieces, and "songs without words." I thought that my imagination produced the result, though it did seem strange that I never heard anything similar in other woods.

Years passed, and I had forgotten all about the matter, when I heard it again, and I will not soon forget the last performance.

Last year I was walking up to X. to drive with Mr. and Mrs. M. to a tennis match. When I reached the usual spot,

78

there burst upon my ear from the direction of the church-yard, what seemed to be the splendid roll of a full brass and reed band. It did not recall the former occasions, and I never for a moment doubted its reality. My first thought was that Sir Y. X. had lent his park for a Sunday-school treat, and my second was that the band was far too good, and the music of far too high a class for such a purpose. I walked on, enjoying it thoroughly, never dreaming that I was not listening to good ordinary music, till it suddenly struck me that the sound, though now faint, ought to have been inaudible, as there was now between me and the churchyard the big broad shoulder of S. (a hill). I began to remember the other—infinitely less distinct—performances I had heard, and though not superstitious enough to believe that there was anything which could not be explained on natural grounds, I felt that the explanation was beyond my power of discovery or conjecture. Of course, I intended immediately telling my friends at X., but my attention must have been called to something else, as I did not do so. We drove away, and after some time, we all, except Mrs. M., got out to walk up a very steep hill. Walking at the side of the carriage I told the most minute circumstances of my strange experience. Mrs. M. seemd to take it very seriously, but Mr. M. ridiculed the whole affair as a freak of the imagination.

I tell you these little incidental circumstances to show you how indelibly the events of the day were engraven upon my memory.

I had not, at that time, heard that the sounds had been listened to by any other person, but it is now well known that they have often been heard by Sir Y. Z. and once by Lady Z.

In the last case the music resembled that of a choir, un-accompanied by instruments. In my cases there was nothing resembling vocal music.

[Signed] J. L. B.

This case was corroborated by other witnesses. Both Lady Z. and her husband, Sir Y. Z., heard chanting and they testify as follows:

On the hot, still afternoon of July 12, 1888, I was sitting resting with some old ladies at our pretty little cemetery chapel, within the grounds of our house in Scotland, far away from all thoroughfare or roads. Whilst I was talking I stopped suddenly and exclaimed, "Listen! what is that singing?" It was the most beautiful singing I had ever heard, just a wave of cathedral chanting, a great many voices, which only lasted a few seconds. The lady said she heard nothing and, thinking she might be deaf, I said nothing. I quite thought it *might* be haymakers at work, and yet I turned my head round, for the singing was so close by. It dawned upon me, "The Scotch need not say they cannot sing." There were several others sitting with us, but they heard nothing (which astonished me). I said nothing more till the evening, when I casually said to my husband, "What was that singing where we were sitting this p.m.?" thinking he would reply, "Oh, it was the men at work." But, to my astonishment, he replied, "I have often heard that before, and it is *chanting* I hear." (Mark, I had not said I had heard several voices, only singing, which was very remarkable.) And then, and not till then, I saw that the voices could not have been human, and certainly I had not imagined it. I had never heard such heavenly (that is the only adjective I can use) music before, and would not have missed it for anything. I was in no wise in a sentimental or fanciful state of mind when I heard the music, but only talking of the common subjects of the day. This is my written statement, and accurately, true.

[Signed] A. Z.

Sir Y. Z. added his corroboration:

When alone at the cemetery I have occasionally heard, from within the chapel, sounds as of chanting.

[Signed] Y. Z.

In these few examples we find a wide assortment of musical

effects. Now, to correlate them to the five theories of hauntings:

The Telepathic Theory: This theory, which confines the outbreaks to the domain of pure subjectivity, involves a group of persons living in a house experiencing psychic precipitation real or hallucinated. As these occupants leave, the new tenants find themselves wrapped in the thoughts created by their predecessors, and they share the experiences. The pattern becomes serialized from tenant to tenant.

The Revised Telepathic Theory: The above explanation handles the total scope of haunting by way of telepathy among the living. The revision of that theory merely extends the range of the telepathy to include the dead—thus hauntings are the result of telepathically produced images from a discarnate agency. The theory would still regard the phenomena as subjective.

The Psychometric Theory: This hypothesis begins to merge with that of the "etheric field" principle. The theory entails believing that, just as objects may retain some impression which may be read clairvoyantly by a "psychometrist," whole houses may be psychometrized and retain the impression of the thoughts and actions of the once living, which may on occasion replay themselves.

The Spirit Hypothesis: The fourth theory accepts the phenomenon *prima facie* that "ghosts" are the "doubles" of the once living which have become rooted to a specified area and that any telekinetic effects are the result of their activity.

The Mental Projection Theory: The last theory of the five is the notion that the living or the dead can set up a tangible life form of themselves which may manifest in a haunting.[1]

Clearly, the first two theories must be discarded. They cannot account for any physical phenomena. Specifically, they do not explain the music heard collectively, which is, after all, the point of this discussion. The psychometric theory does have attractions, especially in the case of the chanting monks, where the phenomena

---

[1] This theory has had a somewhat critical exposition as the persona theory of Professor Hornell Hart (*Enigma of Survival*, Thomas, 1958).

seem to show little motivation, and are repeatedly heard and seen producing the same activities and action. It was from this theory that Professor H. H. Price (Oxford University) structured his "psychic ether" theory of hauntings which he presented as his 1939 presidential address to the S.P.R. Professor Price postulates, as I did in the previous chapter, an intermediate between mind and matter, upon which thought may be impressed, and which may be "picked" or "replayed" as a continuous series of events, and be perceived by sense perception as a haunting.

Ernesto Bozzano, who sparked our initial interest in the whole realm of psychic music, was also an authority on hauntings, and delighted in categorizing their various phenomena. His study is known best to us by its French title, Les Phenomènes de Hantise, which has been translated into English. Bozzano strikes against any psychometric theory on several grounds: (1) Phantoms are seen not only in the area where they lived or died, but in surrounding areas; (2) psychometric theories dare not account for unrelated telekinetic phenomena: raps, footsteps, movement of objects; (3) hauntings often show direct intent and motivation, and have "active" and not "passive" intelligence; (4) the explanation for hauntings should be akin to that for apparitions. (Bozzano offers several other debates on the psychometric theory and its revision but, to my mind, most of them may be met by only minor revision of the initial theory.)

There can be little doubt that many haunting phantoms are to some degree objective—they have been collectively perceived, yet on other occasions are invisible to some but not to others. They have been seen to move matter which was found displaced after the events under observation had taken place, thus proving that this was not part of the psychic phantasm. Music heard in these cases was heard collectively and therefore objective.

Professor Price's theory is good; but it does not go far enough. Many of the characteristics of hauntings do not fit in with being merely revitalized reflections or impressions from a psychic shield. A motion picture camera does set off a nonmaterial figure which may be collectively perceived; but the image cannot influence material objects, nor be seen from different perspectives.

For cases such as the chanting monks, Price's theory is adequate, probably even correct. It has often been argued that hauntings are intermittent; that only certain tenants are prone to vitalize the manifestations. Price's theory overcomes this criticism. Every film needs a proper projector, and not every projector is suitable.

But for more complex cases (such as that of Anne H.) we need more complex theories. Instead of a reflection in the psychic ether, we might actually be faced with a rupture, not just a weakness (as to explain a spontaneous apparition). An apparition is a weakness in the psychic ether; a "ghost" is a continuous apparition; and a haunting is the events around the continuous apparition (though an actual apparition may never be seen) and thus a continuous weakness in the psychic ether. Here the ether takes on more of the properties of matter than of mind.

We have stated that the "vehicle of vitality" functions as the density factor of the "other-world" body. Before a total death experience may take place, any physical properties of the nonphysical body must be ousted. It is generally considered that after death the "vehicle of vitality" is shed. What if, by some freak, this shell does not disintegrate? It may remain plastic and may or may not enslave some portion of the consciousness of the dying. We now have a shell which corresponds to neither the physical nor the "other world," but is a wedge in the psychic ether. Through this wedge we may perceive glimpses of the next world, or perceive its properties (such as "celestial music") with either sense or psychic perception. We may see the shell itself (the "ghost"); or the ether might manifest haphazardly (telekinesis).

It is generally held that hauntings gradually diminish and fade out as time progresses. The famous Morton ghost, one of the best in the records of the S.P.R., grew more feeble until the apparitions and phenomena dissipated. (See Abdy Collins's *The Cheltenham Ghost*, Psychic Press, 1948.) This would be in keeping with our theory, as the rupture gradually rectifies itself.

83

We have spoken of the NAD in its various forms in terms of the "other world," and of the NAD's functions through our only preview of that world—the psychic ether. Since I can explain NAD in no way except by employing this theory, I can only explain hauntings, of which music is an active ingredient, by using this same conceptual scheme. We also answer all of Bozzano's points: (1) We presuppose the survival hypothesis and allow the "ghost" to be a free-acting agent, (2) which, having properties both of this world and the next, can influence physical matter, (3) show intelligence, and (4) explain haunting as a warp in the psychic ether similar to explaining apparitions in terms of "weakness" in the ether.

Chapter 6

NAD, Mystics, and Mediums

All psychical phenomena have certain progenitors easily located within ancient or primitive civilizations, religious doctrine, or common folklore. Mysticism, the belief that man may have direct religious experiences without any intermediaries (such as an established religion or "priestcraft"), being itself supernatural, dovetails in various ways with psychical observation. In fact, the annals of mysticism, in both East and West, are very much impregnated with accounts which we today would classify in the category of psychical phenomena.

It has also been pointed out that the lore of the Roman Catholic saints ties in, to a great extent, with the somewhat more scientifically controlled observations with mediums. Both Saint Ignatius Loyola and Saint Philip Neri had levitations. Saint Thomas Aquinas saw apparitions. With St. Benedict, disembodied voices were heard (the "direct voice" of mediumship). And several have been the target of hauntings—for example, Saint Vianney, Saint Martin, Saint Gemma Galgani.[1]

---

[1] Raymond Bayless, *Enigma of the Poltergeist* (Parker, 1967) pp. 198-208.

These parallels have been so clearly enumerated that some of the Roman Catholic clergy have themselves composed volumes citing common characteristics of both mystics and mediums—surprising, since the Roman Catholic Church has never been overly friendly to parapsychology. Even today the Church is antagonistic to the study of certain phenomena such as precognition. (See Reginald Omez's short book *Psychical Phenomena*, Hawthorn Books, 1958, which comprises Volume 36 of the *Twentieth Century Encyclopedia of Catholicism*. It is listed under Section III, "The Nature of Man," and is more or less an "official" position of modern Catholic views.)

Father Herbert Thurston wrote two books, *The Physical Phenomena of Mysticism* and *Surprising Mystics*, which outline certain psychical features of the lives of the saints. Montague Summers, who was zealously antagonistic to psychics, nevertheless authored *The Physical Phenomena of Mysticism*.

Turning to Asia, we find a counterpart in those experiences attributed to yogis. These too have psychical overtones.

In examining these records, several accounts of celestial music were discovered. Some of these fall into familiar categories—normal states, deathbed cases. However, the outstanding number of them have prompted their inclusion in a self-contained unit. These will be compared to Asiatic doctrines and mediumistic accounts.

Case No. 60 — Saint Guthlac

This case is recounted in Thurston's *The Physical Phenomena of Mysticism* (Burns & Oates, 1952, page 224; American edition, Henry Regnery Co.).

At the death of Saint Guthlac, an observer noted: "When he turned himself again and recovered his breath there came fragrance from his mouth like the odor of the sweetest flowers." His disciple "heard angelic songs through the regions of the air." The first phenomenon, that of supernormal perfume, is the "odor of sanctity," a traditional phenomenon of the saints. Note that the music was described as choral, which parallels modern deathbed observations.

Case No. 61 — Saint Veronica Giuliana

A better-known saint is Saint Veronica Giuliana (1660-1727), who gained beatification because of her "stigmata"—the supernormal (or sometimes hysterical) bleeding at the places where Christ is said to have been nailed to the cross, also the traditional wounds about the head corresponding to Christ's "crown of thorns," and the sword wound in his side.

Saint Veronica Giuliana recorded in her diary on April 5, 1697, the stigmata about her head, visions of Jesus and Mary, and a celestial choir singing "Victory! Victory!" It should be noted that, during OOBE's to which the saints were prone (under the term bilocation—being seen in two places at once), it is traditional that, when apparitions are seen helping to release the "double," they are seen in pairs. While this might seem an exaggeration in this case, the parallel, nonetheless, should be brought out.

Case No. 62 — St. Therese de Lisieux

St. Therese de Lisieux is a relatively contemporary figure, born in 1873 in Normandy. She died in 1897 only twenty-four years later. The case is recorded in Sir Francis Younghusband's *Modern Mystics* (John Murray, 1935). Just before her death she stated:

> Mother, some notes from a distant concert have just reached my ears, and the thought came to me that soon I shall be listening to the music of Paradise.

Case No. 63 — Saint Chad

One of the oldest recorded cases we have is that of Saint Chad, who was bishop of Litchfield, England, and who died in 671. The account is drawn from Omer Englebert's *Lives of the Saints* (David McKay, 1951, p. 84), which reads:

> He died, a victim of the plague, in his beloved Abbey of

Lastingham. A week before, an invisible concert of music had been heard above his cell. Chad opened the window and said to Brother Owen, who was listening in the garden. "That is the angels who are singing, in seven days they will come back to fetch my soul."

Case No. 64 — Saint Joseph of Copertino

Here is the chronicle of the famous saint, Joseph of Copertino, the "flying friar," who was seen to levitate himself at various times during his life (1603-63). The accounts of his death are taken from an excellent résumé of his life in Eric J. Dingwall's *Some Human Oddities* (Home and Von Thal, 1947), which in turn was taken from, among other sources, Bernino's *Vita del P. Fra Giuseppe da Copertino* (1753).

In August, 1663, Joseph was seized by a fever and grew steadily worse. On 17th September, or the day before he died, he received the Viaticum and said he heard the sound of a bell which was summoning him to God. Passing into the ecstatic state he rose from his death bed and flew from his cell as far as the steps of his little chapel. "The Ass is beginning to ascend the mountain," he said, and, having received Supreme Unction, he called out in a loud clear voice, which hardly corresponded with his extreme weakness, "Oh, what chants, what sounds of Paradise."

Several accounts come to us, not only from the annals of recognized saints, but from especially religious Catholics. We recount two here.

Case No. 65 — A Servator

An anonymous case was recorded by Evelyn Underhill in her lengthy volume *Mysticism* (E. P. Dutton & Co., Inc., 1955):

. . . whilst the Servator was still at rest [note that many cases stem from this point, see Chapter 3], he heard within

88

himself a gracious melody by which his heart was greatly moved. And at within him to these words, "Stella Maria maris hode processit ad ortum." That is to say, "Mary Star of the Sea is risen today." And this song which he heard was so spiritual and so sweet, that his soul was transported by it [OOBE?] and he too began to sing joyously. . . .

On another occasion, after the Servator had been at his prayers until dawn, he decided to rest for a short while before beginning his morning devotions:

> . . . whilst his senses were at rest, behold! angelic spirits began to sing to fair respond: "Illuminaire, illuminaire, Jerusalem! . . . The song was echoed with a marvellous sweetness in deeps of his soul. And when the angels had sung for some time his soul overflowed with joy. . . .

Case No. 66 — Richard Rolle

We have some detailed reports of psychic music heard by Richard Rolle, the "Father of English Mysticism" (1290-1349). He studied at Oxford and as a young man decided to devote himself to contemplation. Ultimately he became an inmate of the Cisterian nunnery of Saint Mary (near Doncaster).

Rolle describes the phenomenon in *The Fire of Love* (see David Knowles's *The English Mystical Tradition*, Harper & Row, 1961).

> In searching the Scriptures as best I could I have found and realized that the highest love of Christ consists of three things—fire, song, and sweetness. . . . I call that heat when the mind is truly set on fire with the divine love, and the heart is felt similarly to burn with a love, not in imagination but really. For a heart turned into fire gives the feeling of the fire of love. Song I call it when now the sweetness of eternal praising is received in the soul with abundant heat, and thought is turned into song, and the mind swells upon sweet melody.

89

Rolle compares this heavenly music with earthly music in interesting words (see Evelyn Underhill's *Mysticism* [E. P. Dutton & Co., 1955]).

> . . . for sweet ghostly song accords not with outward song, the which in churches and elsewhere is used. It discords much: for all that is man's voice is formed with bodily ears to be heard; but among angels' tunes it has an acceptable melody, and with marvel it is commended of them that have known it.
>
> . . . . wordly lovers soothe words or ditties of our song may know, for the words they read; but the tone and sweetness of that song may not learn.

More important than doctrine, Rolle gives us his own experiences with the celestial music. Again, these are taken from *The Fire of Love.*

> I was sitting in a certain chapel, and while I was taking pleasure in the delight of some prayer or meditation, I suddenly felt within me an onwonted and pleasant fire. . . . Now from the beginning of this fiery warmth, inestimably sweet, till the infusion of the heavenly, spiritual harmony, the song of eternal praise, and the sweetness of unheard melody, which can be heard and experienced only by one who has received it, and who must be purified and separated from the earth, nine months and some weeks passed away.

A more analytical narrative is also found in the same volume:

> For when I was sitting in the same chapel and was reciting psalms as well as I might before supper, I heard above me the noise of harpers, or rather of singers. And when with all my heart I attended to heavenly things—prayer, I perceived within me, I know not how, a melody and a most delightful harmony from heaven, which abode in my mind.

For my thought was straightway changed into a song, and even when praying and singing psalms I gave forth the selfsame sound. Thenceforth I broke out within my soul into singing what previously I had said. . . .

There are several other instances in Roman Catholic history which are replays of the experiences we have already discussed. Many of these are known to exist but are in extremely obscure texts and could not be incorporated in this volume (some being hundreds of years old, still others never translated from the Latin). In this context Gregory the Great speaks of supernormal music in the lives of Saint Servulus and Saint Romola (Dialogues IV). Saint Severa heard music which was also heard at her deathbed, according to a biography by Stephen, Abbot of St. James (1100).

Traveling to another part of the world, we have some interesting doctrines in Hinduism, which include several forms of yoga: Hatha Yoga (of posture), Gnani Yoga (of knowledge), Raja Yoga (of concentration), Karma Yoga (of good deeds), Bhakti Yoga (of ceremony). That which concerns us is Mantra, or Shabda Yoga, and Kundali Yoga.

Mantra Yoga is based on the concept that the universe is the embodiment of sound, "the audible life stream," and may be attuned to by the repetition of chants (mantras). Kundali Yoga attempts to induce mystic (and psychic) experiences by incorporating the concepts of Mantra Yoga and directing them to open various "psychic centers" (Chakras) of the body.

Within these systems are various doctrines on celestial music. The whole concept of these phenomena is classed under the term NAD (actually NĀDA, the final A being silent). The audible life stream proper is "Shabda." The basic sounds which give rise to the celestial music are the Nada-Bindu. The deity, Brahma, in sound form is Nada-Brahma. The heavenly music is the Akash-bani.

The scriptural doctrines of the NAD may be found primarily in the Nada-Bindu Upanishad of the Rig-Veda. The main point of the Upanishad is a discussion of the "seed sounds" of the celestial music, the "voice of Nada." Other references are scattered in the Yogatattva

Upanishad of the Krishna-Yajur Veda and the Hamsa Upanishad of the S'ukla-Yajur Veda.

Within the Nada-Bindu Upanishad are doctrinal dictates on both the phenomenon and the achievement of its experience. Since the Upanishad would not be comprehensible to those not familiar with Yoga, let me briefly outline it.

The script begins by analyzing the word AUM, which is the embodiment of the Divinity in sound form. The positions of the several Chakras are cited; as are the mantras, which correspond to the awakening of the powers of these psychic organs. Elaborate descriptions are given to the joyous fate of those who die having mastered the secrets of each consecutive Mantra. Upon awakening all the chakras, and having mastered the Mantras, the initiate attains "supreme bliss" and is no longer bound to rebirth.

Upon achieving certain spiritual states, the Upanishad continues, certain sounds will be heard:

> The sound which he thus practices makes him deaf to all external sounds. . . . He hears many loud sounds. They gradually increase in pitch and are heard more and more subtly. At first, the sounds are like those proceeding from the ocean, clouds, kettledrums, and cataracts. In the middle stage those proceeding from mardala, bell, and horn. At the last stage, those proceeding from tinkling bells, flute, vina, and bees.

The Hindu script discusses the ultimate state of the NAD later on in the short Upanishad:

> Just as the bee drinking honey does not care for the odor, so the chitta, which is always absorbed in sound, does not long for sensual objects, as it is bound by the sweet smell of nada, and has abandoned its flitting nature.
>
> The serpent Chitta through listening to the nada is entirely absorbed in it and, becoming unconscious of everything, concentrates itself on the sound.[2]

---

[2] Taken from Narayanaswami Aiyar's translation, *Thirty Minor Upanishads* (Madras, 1914).

After the experience, according to the Upanishad, the consciousness is "above the mind," and all karma (cause and effect) is destroyed and becomes enlightened. In the Dhyanabindu Upanishad, the NAD has the capacity to alleviate sin.

Julian Johnson, who authored a volume on the "audible life stream," *The Path of the Masters* (Punjab, India, Radha Soami Satsang Beas, 1939), describes the traditional view of the NAD as "the grand symphony out of which all other symphonies flow. It is the primal music of the universe. Every musical chord of this world is an echo of that primal chord . . . the all-creative NADA is that sound out of which all other sounds arise, while at the same time its heavenly strains linger in all material worlds as echoes of the original melody." On psychic perception, Johnson states of the NAD, "The original cannot, however, be heard by the physical organ of hearing. A finer sense must be developed for that."

Johnson notes that the same concepts are embodied in Islam as the Sultan-ul-Azkar, talked about by their saints.

To drift away from mysticism, we find our way back to the annals of psychical research and objectively heard music in the presence of mediums.

Case No. 67 — D. D. Home

D. D. Home (1833-86) was one of the first mediums to be tested scientifically. In his early childhood he lived with his aunt, Mrs. McNeil Cook, and resided in both Scotland and the United States. His first psychic experience (according to his autobiography *Incidents in My Life*) was seeing the apparition of his schoolmate, Edwin. His second experience was seeing the apparition of his mother at the same hour that she died.

From that time on, his life was completely overshadowed by his mediumship—soon rappings were heard about him, and similar phenomena. His aunt, believing him demoniacally possessed, threw him out, but scientific interest in him began to be shown (basically because of the raps) by a New York scholar, George Bush. In fact, Professor Wells of Harvard and Professors Hare and Mapes, chemists, became spiritualists after investigating him. Among his diverse phenomena were levitation, movement of objects, immunity to fire, and some materialization phenomena.

The most notable experiments with Home were published privately in 1869 by Lord Adare as *Experiences in Spiritualism with D. D. Home.* This was republished by the Society for Psychical Research many years later.

Home's most famous investigation was conducted by William Crookes, the famed chemist, in 1871. However, all this is well-known material and is recounted in any book on the history of psychical research.

Home recounts in his autobiography the following incident:

> On going to Boston my power returned, and with it the most impressive manifestations of music without any earthly instruments. At night, when I was asleep, my room would be filled as it were with sounds of harmony, and these *gradually grew louder* until persons in other parts of the house could hear them distinctly; if by chance I was awakened, the music would instantly cease.

Lord Adare recorded in *Experiences in Spiritualism with D. D. Home* two cases of psychic music. One was a spontaneous occurrence in July, 1868:

> Almost immediately after we had gone to bed and put the lights out, we both heard the music much the same as at Norwood but more powerful and distinct. Home said that the music formed words; that, in fact, it was a voice speaking and not instrumental music. I could hear nothing but the chords like an organ or harmonium played at a distance.

Later during the experience, Lord Adare heard a choir intone "Hallelujah, praise the Lord; praise the Lord God Almighty" (p. 91).

On a similar occasion in July, 1868, music was heard much in the same fashion:

We had not been in bed more than three minutes when both Home and myself spontaneously heard the music; it sounded like a harmonium, sometimes as if played loudly at a great distance; at other times as if gently, close by. The music continued for some minutes, when Home got up to ask Mr. Jones if any one was playing the accordian. Mr. Jones returned with him and we all three heard the music (page 79).

Case No. 68 — W. Stainton Moses

A medium of a different temperament and caliber was the reserved English clergyman William Stainton Moses (1839-92). Trained at Oxford, he was ordained in the Church of England and began his ministry on the Isle of Man. In 1870 he went to Dorsetshire, and finally in 1871 he received a mastership at the University College School in London, where he remained until 1889, retiring for reasons of health.

The period of his private mediumship was 1872-81. Most of our knowledge of his powers is gained from his friend Dr. S. T. Speer, who administered to him during a serious illness in 1869. Most of Moses's experiences were recorded in his own notebooks, which he handed over to F. W. H. Myers, who published them in the S.P.R. *Proceedings* after his death.

Unlike Home, Moses was not a naturally born psychic, and actually had a stiff dislike for psychic matters. His own mediumship began after his experiences with the medium Lottie Fowler and D. D. Home. He was intent upon developing mediumship more for his own satisfaction that the phenomena existed than for any other goal. Among the phenomena observed with him were the movement of objects, levitation, psychic lights, odors, breezes, and musical sounds.

While Moses did not sit publicly, but only for a few friends, Dr. and Mrs. Speer and F. W. Percival sat with him continually. Among infrequent guests were Serjeant Cox (*What Am I?*) who in 1875 founded the Psychological Society of Great Britain, of which Moses

95

was a member. The association collapsed after Cox's death. William Crookes also witnessed some of the sittings.

The most famous phase of Moses's mediumship was his automatic scripts, which he published anonymously. These were of a philosophical and ethical nature.

His preoccupation with the moral aspects of his own phenomena led him to help found the London Spiritualist Alliance in 1884. He also served on the council of the Society for Psychical Research but, when he felt the Society was becoming overly concerned with the scientific aspects rather than the moral aspects of the study, he resigned.

Most of Moses's marvels were recounted after his death. Of psychic music, Mrs. Speer wrote in *Light*, January 28, 1893:

> On September 19, before meeting this evening we heard fairy bells playing in different parts of the garden, where we were walking. At times they sounded far off, seemingly playing at the top of some high elm trees, music and stars mingling together; then they would approach nearer to us, evidently following us into the séance room which opened on to the lawn.

For many years, hidden within Moses's private notebooks were several references to musical sounds. These came to light when F. W. H. Myers published them in a two-part study, "The Experiences of W. Stainton Moses." (*Proceedings* S.P.R., Volume IX, Part XXXV, and Volume XI, Part XXXVII). Moses wrote of the psychic interplay of two stringed instruments (*Proceedings* IX, page 281).

> They represented two instruments, the one of three, the other of seven strings, and they were used to playing thus: —Certain notes were sounded upon the three strings, and these were followed by a run made as if by running a fingernail rapidly over the strings of the other instrument. The result was like what musical *cognoscenti* call "a free prel-

ude," what I should describe as a series of high notes, highly pitched, clear and of lower pitch. I speak of instruments but . . . there was in the room . . . an ordinary dining room . . . no musical instruments of any kind whatever.

Dr. Speer also recounted hearing plucked notes (*Proceedings* IX, page 281) and goes on to give a description of a different musical phenomenon (page 297).

> . . . imagine the soft tone of a clarinet gradually *increasing in intensity* until it rivaled the sound of a trumpet, then by degrees *diminishing to the original subdued note* of the clarinet, until it eventually died away as a long drawn-out melancholy wail. [Compare with Case Nos. 6, 21.]

Moses himself classified the sounds into nine categories (*Proceedings*, XI, page 54): thick harp string, Egyptian four-stringed harp, three-stringed lyre, seven-stringed lyre, drum roll, ringing of porcelain, high strings of a harp, tambourine, and flapping sounds.

Case No. 69 — Mrs. Chenoweth

In reading over the notes of séances held with the fantastic American medium, Mrs. Chenoweth, by Professor James Hyslop (*Proceedings* A.S.P.R., 1925, "A Further Record of Mediumistic Experiments"), I came across the following conversational fragment. Though nothing is said about the nature of the incident, it nevertheless caught my eye and is here recorded. From the report, Mrs. Chenoweth was ready to go into trance—the parenthesized word is Hyslop's comment:

Did you hear music?

(No)

I wondered if there was an organ outside.

This little extract is suggestive that Mrs. Chenoweth had heard a fragment of psychic music.

Case No. 70 — Thompson-Gifford

One of the greatest case studies in psychic history is the Thompson-Gifford case, which was investigated by Professor James Hyslop, who was for many years the leading light of the American Society for Psychical Research. It was originally published as a huge study in the A.S.P.R. *Proceedings*, and Hyslop wrote a thirty-page summary of it for his last book, *Contact with the Other World* (The Century Co., 1919). The case began in 1905 when Frederic Thompson began to have a compulsive desire to sketch and paint. During these periods he would show remarkable skill in painting with oils and would refer to his second self as Robert Swain Gifford, a gentleman he had casually met several years before. They had met in a marsh where Gifford went to sketch and Thompson to hunt.

In 1906 Thompson read of an exhibition of Gifford's work at the American Art Galleries. On this occasion, for the first time, he discovered that Gifford was dead. (He had died on January 14, 1905, six months prior to Thompson's desire to paint.) From this time forward, Thompson achieved remarkable success at painting, but because of clairaudient experiences (allegedly hearing Gifford's voice) he went to Hyslop for help. At first Hyslop was not impressed by any supernormality of the case. In fact he wrote, "I diagnosed it as disintegrating personality, that is, some type of hallucination and a symptom of mental disturbance."

At this time, however, Hyslop was testing for cases of "obsession" through cross-reference tests with mediums. He would take his patient to various mediums and catalogue their impressions to see if they agreed that the subjects were receiving discarnate impressions. Hyslop took Thompson to a private sensitive, Mrs. Rathbun, who described Gifford and a group of oak trees that Thompson had continually seen clairvoyantly. (Later the actual trees were discovered.)

Thereafter Thompson, being encouraged in his art, attempted to sell his paintings. A Mr. James B. Townsend bought one and independently observed that the painting had an artistic resemblance to Gifford's work.

Next Hyslop took Thompson to Mrs. Chenoweth, and introduced him into the séance room after she had gone into trance. Chenoweth made references characteristic of Gifford and finally to the group of trees mentioned by Rathbun and Thompson. Thompson questioned Chenoweth as to where the trees could be found and the sensitive, then speaking for an unknown communicator (Gifford most likely), gave a description of the trees and the surrounding areas. These proved correct on later investigation.

In June, 1907, Thompson placed a large number of his sketches into the hands of Hyslop and went to search out the areas that Gifford roamed. He met Mrs. Gifford, who took Thompson into her dead husband's studio, where he saw an unfinished sketch, identical to one previously placed in Hyslop's hands. Hyslop writes of this incident:

> The case does not wholly depend on the veracity of Mr. Thompson. He had left the sketch in my hands before he saw the painting by Mr. Gifford. Mrs. Gifford testifies that the picture was rolled up and put away until Mr. Gifford's death, when it was taken out and put on the easel. Mr. Thompson had no opportunity to see it, and his impulse to paint did not arise until six months after Mr. Gifford's death.

Later, in traversing privately owned islands off the New England coast, Thompson recognized several of his clairvoyant visions, some of which he had sketched. Hyslop subsequently verified these areas himself.

This is only part of this complex case. Several attempts to communicate with Gifford through private sensitives were made; many of these essays were blessed with highly veridical and evidential material.

As for music, along with many clairvoyant experiences there were clairaudient encounters, such as hearing Gifford's voice. Hyslop, in his summary of the case in *Contact with the Other World*, devotes one paragraph to Thompson's musical clairaudience:

Mr. Thompson had many other interesting experiences which he recorded in his diary at the time. When he was on the island searching for the scenes which had haunted his visions, he often heard music like that of a guitar or violin, and hunted about to see if it was produced by any one. He found no evidence of any human cause. In fact, there seems to be but one house on the island, except the three or four at the Eastern end of it. The island has no population except two or three families of care-takers. Besides, this music was heard at different times and places on the island and once Mr. Thompson ran up a hill to see if he could find someone whom he fancied he heard singing, but found no one. *Usually the music he heard was instrumental* [corresponding to mediumistic persons, see Chapter 3]. A friend of Mr. Gifford states that Mr. Gifford was passionately fond of music, especially the violin. Whether there is anything more than a coincidence in this circumstance must be determined by each one for himself.

There is a subsequent note to this music. On April 10-11, 1907, sittings were held with Mrs. Chenoweth, who came up with several evidential statements about Gifford and Thompson. Then she gave several statements to the effect that "discarnates" were trying to draw Thompson from his body, and Thompson admitted having experiences very similar to the OOBE. Finally, Chenoweth states, ". . . you have a sort of hearing. It is not definitely unfolded yet, but there are times when you get strains of music, just as though it floats about you."

Case No. 71 — Reine

The records on Reine are taken from an interesting book *Survival of the Soul* by Pierre-Emile Cornillier (Kegan Paul, 1921). Cornillier, an artist, discovered that Reine, his model, had mediumistic ability and further that she was a good mesmeric subject. Through her "communicator," Vettellini, Cornillier recorded several philosophical and "spirit" teachings, plus a guide to the further development of

100

Reine's ability. Twice Cornillier noted that Reine, during her "fluidic state" (trance) heard astral music. (He was also able to exteriorize her double.) On page 246 of his volume, Cornillier notes:

> She tells me that in her actual fluidic state she surely would not have been able to discern these extraordinary astral delights, but she was aided, her perceptions were rendered more sensitive and she became spiritualized to the point of being conscious of harmonics so marvellous that no language can express them. She is obliged to use the term "music"; it is the word which, for us, corresponds the most closely to the cause of the enchantment which still holds her in strong emotion. But what a poor, thin, little word it is!—How toneless!—How inadequate to convey the intensity of that thrilling harmonious vibration.

On page 252, Cornillier records another magnetic session with Reine:

> At the last séance Vettellini ordered only a good training exercise for Reine today, and, in consequence, I magnetized for about an hour and a half, attempting no experiment, and waiting for her to come of her own accord to the phase of transmission. She reaches out her hands, verifies me, so to speak, and begins her report. There was another concert today, up there, where the blue spirits live, and she could again rejoice in those harmonies which had so enchanted her once before.

Of main interest in this case is that Vettellini, the *soi-disant* communicator, himself commented upon celestial music, which several observers have attributed to the activities of the discarnates. He states as to the music's production:

> Obviously spirits have no musical instruments to play upon, but they can create and combine innumerable vibrations giving the most marvellous sensations of music and

101

poetry. You, the incarnated, have but the mere suggestion, the faintest echo of what it really is.

Discussing Vettellini's "teachings," Cornillier writes about the musical properties of the "other world":

They, the spirits, can travel throughout all space, observe the revolution of worlds and assist their phenomena. Musical harmonies are a source of never-ending pleasure for them. They have no instruments, evidently,—they have no need for them. It is in combining vibrations that they create what is the very essence of the harmonies of sound that we call music, and often they meet together for this purpose.

Such communications are indeed naïve, and one knows not what to make of them. Similar remarks have come through other mediums, notably to the S.P.R.'s famous and well-investigated medium, Mrs. Gladys Osborne Leonard. During the famous communications recorded by Sir Oliver Lodge communicating with his son, Raymond, which included evidential material as well as much descriptive matter, Raymond stated, "There are places on my sphere where they [spirits] can listen to beautiful music when they choose. Everybody, even here, doesn't care for music, so it's not in my sphere compulsory." (*Raymond*, Methuen, Ltd., 1916.)

C. Drayton Thomas records, through Mrs. Leonard, these words from her celebrated control Feda about the status of the arts in the "other world." "Of the arts, music and painting come first, and music takes premier place." (*Life beyond Death with Evidence*, William Collins' Sons, 1928.)

As an interesting comparison, the Tibetan doctrines have a similar view of music in the after-life, W. Y. Evans-Wentz writes in "Yoga of the After-death State" in his volume *Tibetan Yoga and Secret Doctrines* (Oxford University Press, 1958). The excerpt discusses the departure of the consciousness from the body at death via any of nine "doors" of the body. Evans-Wentz in the Tibetan script states:

In the case of a person dying yogically untrained, the departure of the consciousness ordinarily takes place through some of these "doors" [corresponding to the eyes, ears, nostrils, etc.] each "door" leading to a birth in that non-human state to which it corresponds. For instance, the departure through the "door" of one of the ears leads to birth in the world of the Gandharvas (fairylike celestial musicians) where-in musical sound is the prevailing quality of existence.

By way of coincidence, according to the Nadabindu Upanishad, the NAD is heard through the right ear only.

It is hard to analyze this last group of material. Did experience lead to doctrine, or is there some metaphysical reality to these documents? I can not pretend to judge.

Aside from the phenomenal effects witnessed by those selected few who sat with Home and Moses, several other mediums have had slight manifestations of musical effects—usually single or random notes. While not so fascinating as the astral choirs and psychic harmoniums of Home, nevertheless such small phenomena must hold our attention. Even the Akash-Bani of the Hindus is but a growth from the Voice of NADA, the "seed sounds."

Case No. 72 — Margery

Never has controversy—and scandal—been more the concern of parapsychology than the mishandled case of Mina Stinson, known to her psychic public as "Margery," the wife of the Boston physician, Dr. L. R. G. Crandon. After her husband's interest in psychical phenomena had been kindled, Margery's own mediumship developed—raps, automatic writing, and finally "direct voice." Later . . . telekinesis and materialization. There was a formidable array of scientists and investigators who made her their concern—William McDougall, W. Franklin Prince, Hereward Carrington, Gustav Geley, even J. B. Rhine. All held different opinions both as to her phenomena and her character.

103

In 1924, Margery attempted to win the award offered to any physical medium who could satisfy the judges of the *Scientific American* Magazine. The fiasco which followed, with the internal squabbling that resulted, was both amusing and infamous.

J. Malcolm Bird, who was not the ideal investigator, set himself up as Margery's champion and wrote a volume about her, *Margery, the Medium*. He also edited a favorable report in the *Proceedings* of the A.S.P.R.; though it can hardly be said that the A.S.P.R. had a highly critical attitude toward psychical research at the time. It had, in fact, badly disintegrated after the death of James Hyslop some years before. Nevertheless the annals of the mediumship are interesting reading (if one can wade through Bird's boring style) and can provide us with a diversity of musical sounds.

One musical sound noted by Bird was gentle taps "as on a bell so pure as to bear no vibration, in the most exquisite tones, quite beyond description."

Also heard were notes as if a piano were being struck, some sort of harmonica, and strikings on what Bird calls "the celestial clock."

Case No. 73 — Mrs. Blake

Buried within the annals of psychical research are many records much in necessity of being "rediscovered." One of these is a report on an old, crippled "trumpet medium" in Ohio, who died in 1920. Mrs. Blake sat in daylight with a two-foot trumpet and merely held the cone to the sitter's ear. From the cone emanated whispers, gradually building into loud voices which could be heard across a room. All the while Mrs. Blake sat in her wicker chair, stoically staring into space. I have seen a picture taken during one of these sittings and it is a bit humorous—an old, crippled woman, staring straight ahead into space, with a group of elegantly dressed savants observing her for treacherous fraud (which was never found) and eagerly listening into her magic trumpet.

But the results were anything but amusing. The great conjurer David Abbott, who wrote the condemning *Behind the Scenes with the Mediums,* a textbook on psychic fakery, became convinced of her authenticity, as did another conjurer, E. A. Parsons.

Aside from a few notes in Isaac J. Funk's *The Psychic Riddle* (Funk & Wagnall's, 1907), the only source for the study of Mrs. Blake is a lengthy report by James Hyslop and collaborators, who also accepted the genuineness of the phenomena. Other than the mere production of the voices, much evidential material—including proper names—was given by the voices (*Proceedings* ASPR, Volume VII, pages 570-788).

I came across this report when doing a study of "direct voice" mediumship. On one occasion, instead of voices coming from the trumpet, there emanated piano music!

The production of piano music with Blake ties in with Margery and with keyboard music heard with Home. We do not know the extent of the music since the experimenters note it only in passing, and only quite by accident did it catch my eye.

Case No. 74 — Attila von Sealay

One medium of this same experimental genre is Attila von Sealay, an American of Hungarian extraction. I have been able to experiment with the medium, and a short summary of previous work with him was published by Raymond Bayless in the *Journal* A.S.P.R., 1959, Volume LIII, No. 1.

Von Sealay claims to have heard the NAD twice (in fact, it was he who introduced me to the yogic side of the phenomenon).

As to individual music sounds, we have the following account, which has never before been published. The statements of those concerned were taken from Mr. Bayless's file. This is Von Sealay's statement:

> On July 18, 1956, I was lying in bed when I heard a series of flutelike sounds, I held my breath, listened, and found they were about one foot from my face. I heard the sounds for about ten to fifteen minutes. I was going to call Mr. Bayless' attention to this phenomenon (he had stayed at my

studio overnight) but was afraid it might be inhibited in its action or disappear entirely if I did so. It was a sweet, silvery tone, but played notes at random rather than a melody. I encouraged it to increase in amplitude, but to no avail. As I made an effort to reach the tape recorder on the other side of the room, the sounds diminished and finally died away entirely. While I was listening, it would play and cease intermittently. Apparently any movement would disturb it. After Mr. Bayless awakened, I related these events to him. When we went out to have breakfast, Mrs. Consetta Marro (who had shown mediumistic ability and with whom we have been experimenting), who worked at this restaurant, came to our table. I asked her if anything unusual had occurred to her last night and she replied that nothing happened except that she had heard a flute playing. I questioned her as to the melody it played without revealing that I had heard the same sounds. She then told me that it did not play a melody, but just sounded notes at random. She whistled in an attempt to emulate the sounds, and I was pleasantly surprised to find that they were practically identical with the notes I had heard.

Mrs. Marro wrote out her own statement as follows:

On the morning of July 18, 1956, Mr. Attila von Sealay and Mr. Raymond Bayless came into the restaurant where I work and ordered breakfast. When I came to their table to take their orders, Mr. Von Sealay asked me if anything unusual had happened during the night. I then described a very strange event which had taken place. About 1:00 or 1:30 a.m. I heard a flute being played. It sounded various notes but did not play a melody. I had not gone to bed at the time but was in my living room.

In analyzing all these testimonies we may make three important observations:

The Universality of the Phenomenon: It has often been claimed that in order to be accepted, it must be shown that psychic phe-

106

nomena occur in a variety of cultures and are not just a cultural artifact of our own. We have shown that the NAD has been known not only in parapsychological literature, but in the lore of the saints and the ancient Indian culture. No significant differences in the data have appeared within these three sets of case studies.

The Composite Nature of the Phenomenon: All psychical phenomena are composite in nature. Within the boundaries of mental phenomena, we begin with telepathy; by dismissing the "agent" we are gripped by a more complex phenomenon—clairvoyance. Extending its time boundaries, we have precognition. Finally, destroying all theoretical boundaries, we have the species in its most complex form—trance mediumship. The same may be said for telekinesis, which from influencing the fall of dice (psychokinesis), builds the power to move objects, levitate tables, and (the force becoming visible) manifest as materializations. The NAD is of this same nature—from single musical notes it builds into harmoniums, orchestras, and choirs. The same characteristics of the phenomena were noted by Hindu scholars two thousand years ago. NAD neatly fits into the organizational plan of other psychical phenomena.

Spontaneous and Controlled Genres: It may safely be said that every spontaneous phenomenon has a mediumistic counterpart. Telepathy which, with *Phantasms of the Living* and the *Census of Hallucination,* began as a field study now has been caged in the laboratory by the work of the quantitative school of parapsychology pioneered by J. B. Rhine, who with testing have partially controlled precognition and clairvoyance with selected subjects; not to mention the work done with Piper and Leonard.

The noisy rattlings of the poltergeist and similar haunting effects are also produced by physical mediums. The NAD has manifested both spontaneously in haunting and with individuals and, under control, with mediums Home and Moses.

As we proceed, the NAD takes on, more and more, the capacity and properties of an individual psychical phenomenon, and one that has been sadly neglected.

107

Chapter 7

NAD — Some Further Cases

Approaching a topic such as psychic music creates several problems. As has been suggested, one of the basic problems is that of categorization. Several of our cases might be classified either as OOBEs or related to death. Dovetailing is found in any comprehensive system, and there is always the inconvenient log of cases that really do not fall into any clear category, and which could have easily been omitted from this monograph. However, there are certain oddities that, from a standpoint of intellectual honesty, must be reported.

In this chapter we shall present some diverse cases which could have been placed in other chapters, but all of which have certain unique characteristics worthy of special attention.

As is obvious from the structure of this book, I felt it necessary that before psychic music could be considered as an individual phenomenon, an understanding of the OOBE should be introduced simultaneously with it. It had been shown that the patterns of the NAD nearly always correspond to those of the OOBE—and this judgment was formed by the study of spontaneous cases. As a singular psychical talent (the OOBE) we should expect to find several individuals who seem to have an affinity for the phenomenon—

persons who continually report the experience. And, of course, several persons have — Sylvan Muldoon, Oliver Fox (pseudonym), "Yram," Professor Whiteman, and others (see Appendix B). It is also probable that several persons habitually hear psychic music.

This theme is well brought home in an excellent little article entitled "Transcendental Music" by James Doughty, published in the English journal *Light* (September, 1945).

Mr. Doughty opens his article by quoting what could be called a case of a habitual percipient. Notice the contemplative psychological setting and its similarity to cases such as Bayard Taylor reported earlier. The woman, in her naïveté, had written the author expressing the desire to know whether others had reported such experiences:

Case No. 75 — A Lonely Child

When a child of six or seven, or possibly later, I was much alone, amusing myself in a very large garden, and amongst trees and shrubberies. I have enjoyed being alone with nature where it seems one can feel the nearness of the Divine. It seemed no surprise, at this age, that I contacted very lovely music. I just stood still and absorbed it, and it made such a deep and lasting impression that I have never lost its perfect satisfaction. Depending upon no notes [note that most of the cases are not defined as having a melody, but more often pure sensuous sound], it filled my being with harmony and joy . . . [dots are Doughty's] The music I experienced was not exactly *heard*, it was *perceived*, and seemed four-dimensional, solid, filling my very being.

Many persons have recorded having "other-world experiences" during such states. We have cited the case of Bayard Taylor; and even the great psychical researcher and scholar, F. W. H. Myers, seems to have had an OOBE during a similar state. Further, cases such as the preceding indicate that the ability to hear transcendental music may not be a momentary "glimpse into eternity," but a controllable and even developable (and habitual) experience.

On the other side of the spectrum we find that distraught, uneasy states of mind do not *induce* natural OOBE's but rather *enforce* them. We find this next case also in Mr. Doughty's article. It was submitted to him by a newspaper writer:

Case No. 76 — A Newsman

My mind was an arid desert, unfertile, and unproductive of ideas. Suddenly in the midst of such cognition I was astonished to find my room flooded with the musical strains of an extraordinary fine orchestration. I sprang to my feet and threw open the windows overlooking the river. It was midnight and all was calm and serene in that rural retreat. . . . "Where could this music have come from?" I asked myself. I knew there was no musical instrument in my own establishment beyond an ordinary piano, and my neighbors were too far removed to be heard, even in the improbable eventuality of their desiring music at that unconventional hour of the night. I hastily closed the window and once more seated myself at my desk. *Within a few seconds the orchestration had commenced in full volume and beauty.* It was obvious then that no ordinary house instrument could have produced such a massed effect. And remember, this was many years ago, long before broadcast entertainments or wireless concerts were within the range of practical adaptability.

Convinced that I must be under a misapprehension as to the place from which the music emerged, I went to the window again, but no sooner had I thrown it open than the music stopped and nothing but the silence of the night confronted me. The music remained in my study. Immediately I removed myself from the room it came to an end. I had then (although I confess I was sceptical) a hazy impression of some occult demonstration.

Here again we find a complete corroboration between OOBE-inducing states of consciousness and NAD-inducing states of consciousness. The narrative also contains several other interesting sidelights: As with so many other cases this incident took place late at night, when the physical condition of the organism is at lowest ebb (and, according to occult lore, the "astral body" is in need of revitalization). Through my correspondence I have been able to send out questionnaires to many persons having this experience and, while hardly enough to make any detailed analysis, most of them had the experience in the evening . . . but they emphatically state they were not dreaming. The results of this questionnaire will be mentioned as this chapter progresses.

Mr. Doughty's categorization of transcendental music was similar to my own (though mine was structured independently of it). His listings are as follows: (1) Music heard at deathbeds either by the dying or by deathbed observers, (2) music heard during sickness, (3) music heard in circumstances not related to illness or death, (4) music heard in the presence of mediums, and (5) music heard during the playing of a musical instrument but extraneous to the sound being produced.

Case No. 77 — Charles E. Hicks

Cases related to death and illness are perhaps the commonest of all. And so it is with OOBEs. This case, taken from *Fate* Magazine (April, 1967), is an oddity, and it is difficult to tell whether it was an "enforced" or "natural" projection:

> On a Sunday evening in May, 1950, I suffered a ruptured appendix following an attack of food poisoning. I knew I was in serious trouble and resigned myself to whatever might happen after the emergency surgery. I awakened in my hospital room at 11:00 p.m. I recognized my wife standing near my bed, then passed into coma. During these critical comatose hours the visions appeared. . . . As a "spectator" I saw myself lying unconscious on a hospital bed. In another part of the "stage" I was standing at the gateway to another world. Somehow I knew the man at the gate, the doorway to eternity, wasn't real. He was an image of the man on the bed but composed of some ethereal

111

substance. Stretching out before me (in my role as gate-keeper) I could see a broad white expanse—a field of cotton batting. In the distance a range of low goldtipped hills stood sharp against a clear blue sky. *From somewhere beyond the hills came the sound of a choir singing in a strange tongue.* A brilliant morning sun lighted the blue sky above the hills. I wanted to walk into the sun—but a voice from beyond bade me go back to finish something I had left undone. [Refer to the many instances of this in the second chapter.] I turned and walked into a black void that rose like a high wall around me [the "tunnel" effect].

Case No. 78 — Ruth Hall

Another case of near-death is that of Ruth Hall, who wrote in *Fate* (June, 1960) of her OOBE. She had entered a Texas hospital to have an appendectomy in 1936. After a short recuperation she was ready to be dismissed from the hospital but she suffered a hemorrhage and fell into unconsciousness:

I found myself in a strange place, a land of indescribable beauty, unlike any place I had ever known [paradise condition]. It was a land of green meadows and blossoming trees; the air was softly sweet and fragrant and diffused with a rosy glow. All about me was the most *glorious music—muted rapturous harmony.* I felt supremely happy, exalted, complete.

Mrs. Hall goes on to say that she then saw across a stream the figures of her yet incarnate husband and children [this is quite common—perceiving water separating the "earth" and "other-world" conditions] and knew she must go back to them. She then recovered consciousness.

Case No. 79 — R. K. Beggs

The following incident occurred in 1929 when Mr. Beggs attempted to save a child from drowning. It was recorded in *Fate* (March, 1960):

Suddenly a mountainous wave broke over me. I went down, down, down, into the quiet depths of the dark water. . . . It seemed then that a wonderful transition occurred. I was no longer in the water but rather I was high above the water and looking down upon it. The sky, that had been so grey and lowering, was now iridescent with indescribable beauty. *There was music that I seemed to feel* rather than hear. [Note that this is concordant with our hypothesis that music in enforced OOBEs is not as brilliant as in natural ones.] Waves of ecstatic and delicate color vibrated around me and lulled me to a sense of peace beyond comprehension.

Later Mr. Beggs found himself staring at his own body, losing consciousness, and being brought back to awareness by lifeguards.

Case No. 80 — Julia Roupp

In OOBEs and death experiences, discarnates have actually been seen singing, as in the following account which was originally published in *Guideposts,* October, 1963, and incorporated into Susy Smith's *The Enigma of out-of-Body Travel* (Garrett Publications, 1965):

Mrs. Julia Roupp of Minneapolis, Minnesota, during a thyroid operation, suddenly found herself looking down at herself and the doctors and nurses from a short distance over their heads. She heard the anesthetist say that her pulse was going and she started through what seemed to be a long, dark passageway. As she went along she thought calmly, "This must be what they call dying." This journey continued uneventfully for some time . . . but finally she found herself looking into an enormous convex window. "I knew it was not glass," she says, "for I could easily have stepped through to the other side, at the same time the thought came to me that I must be looking through a window into one bright spot of Heaven. What I saw there made all earthly joys pale into insignificance." She was delighted then to see a merry throng of children singing and frolicking in an apple orchard, and she longed to join them. Then she became aware of a presence of joy, harmony and compassion which was beside her. Her heart yearned to become a part of this beauty but somehow she could not bring herself to go through the window. "An invisible, tenacious restraint pulled me back each time I leaned forward with that intention." After a time she returned to her body and then, during the next twenty-four hours, while she was in a critical condition, "All the meanings of life and death seemed to pass before my inner eyes."

It has often been said that such examples as these are explainable as hallucinations, thus the evidence for out-of-the-body experiences rests in citings of "apparitions of the living." To prove that NAD is not hallucinatory, a great amount of evidence, based on collectively perceived cases by unsuspecting observers, must be collected. The next case is one in which music was heard objectively. However, instead of choral music, which is usually the case, organ music was perceived. (Comparisons of the NAD to the strains of an organ, usually with a choir, have been quite prolific in the narratives of this book.) This case is taken from *Light*, October 19, 1881. The narrator was a physician:

Case No. 81 — A Shopkeeper and His Wife

One day, my patient said, while in a little parlour behind the shop he heard music so loud that he thought an organ was being played at the open street door. Preparing to go and shut it, he heard his wife calling from the kitchen stairs, asking him to send the organ man away, for the sake of a sick lodger, with whom she had much sympathy. The street door was not open, and now the music sounded from above. "My wife hastened up the stairs," he said, "and I, as mystified as she was, followed, for we knew there was neither musician nor musical instruments in the house except my own violin, hanging up in the parlour. The door of the sick woman's bedroom was ajar, and my wife, who frequently visited her, pushed it open and with a gesture of wonder beckoned to me. There was the sick woman, lying in bed, gazing upwards, her hands raised as if in rapt astonishment, the music sounding within the room. Presently the hand fell, *the music died away as if in the distance,* and then we saw that she had ceased to breathe."

My patient's wife was present and confirmed the narrative as it went on. They said they were unable to account for the music, and felt driven to the conclusion that it was unearthly.

Many of the cases so far recorded in this chapter indicate that the music was heard from a fixed point in space. This was confirmed by my own correspondents, who usually stated that they felt the music to be located in a spatial relationship.

Psychic music may play a role in forms of psychical experiences other than the "other-world" type. For instance, precognition:

Case No. 82 — C. M. Dyer

C. M. Dyer (Dorset, Great Britain) sent me this odd and fascinating account of his witness to psychic music (November, 1968):

About the year 1920 when I was fifteen, I lived with my parents and sister in Frome, a quiet country town in Somerset. One night during the winter I had gone to bed in a room in front of the house while my parents and sister were still up and talking at the rear of the house. The time was about 10:30. I was not asleep, but *suddenly heard a strange kind of music, which quickly grew louder and then faded away* as if it was passing by in the wood outside. There was, however, no other sound, such as a vehicle would have made. And this was before the days of radio. It lasted, I suppose, about ten to fifteen seconds and had a peculiar quality, like tinkling bells with probably flutes and dulcimers. The impression I received can only be described as if it was "faery" music. In the morning I mentioned it to my parents, but I think they ascribed the experience to a dream.

115

However, the following evening we were all together in the front room, at about the same time, when the same music was heard by all four of us, so proving it to be objective. I quickly went to the front door, but before I reached it the sound had ceased and nothing was to be seen or heard.

There is a sequel. . . . About four or five years ago I was looking through the radio programs and noted that the B.B.C. was to broadcast an adaptation of *The Lord of the Rings*, a somewhat esoteric novel or fairy tale by J. Tolkien. I decided to listen and was amazed when I heard the introductory music, which I immediately recognized as the same "faery" music I had heard so many years ago.

This case may be approached from many angles. We could dismiss it altogether as a clever piece of fiction. However, note the familiar crescendo and decrescendo of the music. Also, the narrator notes the fifteen-second length of the music. Several other correspondents who returned their questionnaires to me also calculated the experience to have lasted for about this same duration.

If, in fact, we can hear music of the future—could not we hear music of the past? Certain haunting cases strike a note of "retrocognition"—for example, chanting monks—but one case worthy of deep analysis is the famous *An Adventure*.

Case No. 83 — Moberly and Jourdain

Every student, or even casual peruser, of psychic lore is familiar with the case of the Misses Moberly and Jourdain, who under the pseudonyms of "Miss Morison" and "Miss Lamont" wrote of their experiences in *An Adventure* (1911), which had numerous printings.[1]

The two ladies, while walking in Versailles, suddenly found themselves transported in time to the Versailles of pre-French revolutionary days and witnessed scenes and costumes of that period.

---

[1] One of the best is by Faber & Faber, 1948, to which reference is made here.

After the phantasmic experience was over, the two women, very highly thought of English educators, painstakingly sought to check historical maps and data on the area they had visited to verify their visions with historical fact. The results make up one of the most controversial cases in psychic history. The implications and complexity of the case are too involved to analyze in this volume, and the experience tends to be related to "hauntings." (I doubt whether there was actually a "transportation in time," and prefer to view the case on a psychical level.)

The Society for Psychical Research was adverse to the case, although Sir William Barrett, around whose work the S.P.R. was founded, finally acknowledged its authenticity after initially holding hostile views. He was later joined in his opinion by Andrew Lang and Sir Oliver Lodge.

The Versailles case occurred in 1901. In January, 1902, Miss Jourdain returned to the Petit Trianon in Versailles to see if this phenomenon would repeat itself. It did. Included in her second experience was the hearing of music:

> The crowd got scarce and drifted away and then faint music as of a band [a string band], not far off, was audible. It was playing very light music with a good deal of repetition in it. Both voices [of the crowd] and music were diminished in tone, as in a phonograph, unnaturally. The pitch of the band was lower than usual. The sounds were intermittent and once more I felt the swish of a dress close by me.

During both of these "adventures" the retrocognition of the past was preluded by a peculiar feeling of oppression.

After the incident, Miss Jourdain, to whom Edith Olivier refers (in her preface to the 1948 edition) as a "brilliant musician," wrote out twelve bars of the music, or at least a skeleton outline of the basic melodic and harmonic lines.

In 1908 Miss Jourdain verified that no outdoor bands had been allowed to play in Versailles until 1907 and that no outdoor park

117

concerts would be audible at Trianon.

In the first edition of the book it was stated that an unnamed musical expert had expressed his opinion that the music was of the idiom of about the late eighteenth century, and that the music could have been written by Sacchini. He further found one harmonic error in Miss Jourdain's dictation.

In *An Adventure* we read further:

> In the same month they [Miss Jourdain and anonymous friend] searched through a great deal of unpublished music in the Conservatoire de Musique at Paris and discovered that the twelve bars represented the chief motives of the light opera of the eighteenth century, excluding Rameau and his school, and that, as far as they could discover, nothing like them occurred in the opera of 1815 onward. Such passages were found in Sacchini, Philidor, Monsigny, Gretry, and Pergolesi. Grammatical mistakes were found in Monsigny and Gretry.

As for musical literature, Jourdain proposed Sacchini's two operas *Dardanus* and *Oedipe a Colone*, various pieces of Philidor ("Regaudons" and *Le Marechal Ferrand*). Dumi, Monsigny's *Le Roi et le Fermier* and *Le Deserteur*, Gretry's operas, and Pergolesi's *Largo* and *Andante in D* were also included.

And that is where the *An Adventure* case rested for many years —the actual music was conspicuously never published and the anonymous "music expert" was not identified.

However, in 1966 a reanalysis of the music, taking into account both its musicology and psychical relevancy, was published as a monograph, *The Music of "An Adventure"* (London, Regency Press, 1966) by Professor Ian Parrott, the English composer and professor of music at the University College of Wales.

For the first time the actual music is published—a short, rather uninteresting twelve-bar progression in A flat major.

One of the key issues of Professor Parrott's analysis is Miss Jourdain's statement that the music was "low in pitch," although she

118

had not previously heard the exact selection. Professor Parrott writes:

> If music is flat to the amount of one semitone, it might be argued that it will not sound out-of-tune but merely in another key. This argument cannot be supported by a thoughtful musician, nor even by Miss Jourdain, despite her modesty regarding her musical ear. Her remark about the phonograph comes in here. There is an unnatural "flatness," which is not the same as music played in a lower key. Also if the music is played by a string band, the musical ear will expect certain keys in which the open strings resonate well in sympathy. A piece for strings in A major played slowly on a modern Gramophone (no less than the old phonograph) in the key of A flat major will sound wrong. It will not sound the same as a piece written in the less resonant key of A flat major.

The gist of the argument leads us to the fact that today (since 1939) the concert pitch is standardized at the tuning of A440. In Miss Jourdain's era the A was tuned to 439 cycles per second. At the critical period we are discussing, the music of the eighteenth century, the standardized tuning was about A422. Thus it is not at all surprising that Miss Jourdain heard an unnatural lowness to the music. Professor Parrott also points out that A flat major could have been a "depressed" perception of A major, which was a quite common key signature at that time, while A flat major was uncommon then.

The heavier section of Professor Parrott's booklet is devoted to a musical analysis of the various suggested sources of the twelve bars offered by Miss Jourdain—all of which he criticizes.

Most of Professor Parrott's conclusions are musicological; however, he does show a great deal of insight into the relationship of the aural and visual phenomena which took place at Versailles. Anne Moberly, who accompanied Miss Jourdain, gives us a precise description of her visual perception of the new world she discov-

119

ered; and Miss Jourdain gives the particulars of the aural phenomena:[2]

Visual Phenomena	Aural Phenomena
1. "Unnatural, unpleasant"	"Eerie and oppressive"
2. "Flat and lifeless"	"Diminished in tone"
3. "No effects of light and shade"	"Faint music—the pitch of the band lower then usual"
4. "The general impression of a stage set"	"Compared to a phonograph"

Indeed the relationship between the interweaving of the visual and aural perceptions is above chance; and Professor Parrott is to be congratulated on a most worthwhile endeavor. Nevertheless, the monograph did set off quite a correspondence war in the *Journal* of the S.P.R. The book was reviewed by the eminent musician Rollo Myers (who has recently written a book on Erik Satie). He reiterated his negative view of the case in a letter to the *Journal* S.P.R., March, 1968:

> . . . But I still maintain that to say of a piece of unfamiliar eighteenth-century music that its pitch was "lower than usual" is meaningless unless the hearer had heard it played before at a higher pitch. In this case she would have been able to identify the music.

I find Mr. Myers's comment naïve. Any individual with "relative pitch" (closely akin to perfect pitch) can easily perceive when a piece of music is being played at a lower pitch. Mr. Myers's flaw is that he is still assuming the issue to be the key in which the composition was played rather than the pitch discrepancies between A439 and A422.[3]

---

[2] See page 45 of *The Music of "An Adventure."*

[3] Some of Rollo Myers's comments on the case other than the music aspect have been challenged by Andrew McKenzie (*Journal* S. P. R., December, 1967).

It really makes no difference *what* is being played. Any musician, professional or amateur, can easily hear a pitch discrepancy. Myers, like the music critic Ernest Newman, who used the criticism in 1912, has simply missed the point of the case.

The Reverend J. P. Hill, in order to clarify the problem, has suggested perhaps Miss Jourdain meant to write that the "key" of the music, not the "pitch" was too low (*Journal* S.P.R., December, 1967). But this is challenged by Rollo Myers (*Journal* S.P.R., March, 1968), who still maintained the same argument that the necessity of having previously heard the music holds true for either key or pitch. (In fact, the quote from Myers, used to sum up his verdict of the case, is extracted from his reply to the Reverend Hill.) On the other hand Professor Parrott himself remarks (*Journal* S.P.R., March, 1968): "The point I make in my book, however, is one which can be appreciated only by someone who is able to distinguish between sounds in the 'real' world and those in the world of dreams or hallucination."

The above quotation refers to Professor Parrott's comment that he was dreaming of listening to music and woke up to hear a piano being played. He noted that the "dream music" was flat in relation to it. From this, Professor Parrott suggests that perhaps all "dream music" is flat. Since the sleep state is somewhat akin to a trance state, and seems to be a state of consciousness during which psychic perceptions more easily take root, the "flatness" of the "dream music" may well be akin to "hallucinatory" music or, indeed, all "psychic music." (The term "hallucinatory" is not meant to be used negatively.)

I think the whole controversy was well summed up by Professor J. H. M. Whiteman (whom we have dealt with before in connection with "other-world" experiences) in his comments on *The Music of "An Adventure."* I think it well worthwhile to reproduce his entire letter to the *Journal* S.P.R., June, 1968. Professor Whiteman wrote:

In support of the Revd. J. P. Hill's view, in a letter published in the December *Journal*, that "less than justice" has been done to Miss Jourdain in the matter of the Versailles music, I should like to put forward some further considerations which I think favour the attribution of retrocognitive character to the experience.

I take it as clear that when Miss Jourdain wrote "the pitch of the band was lower than usual" she could not have meant "usual for this particular piece" as Ernest Newman and Rollo Myers have supposed, but that she meant something like "usual for a piece of that type as heard on instruments of today." For proof that a piece that one has never heard before may give the indubitable impression of being at a "lower pitch than usual" reference may be made to the Suite in E minor by J. S. Bach, printed in Vol. VII of the Steingraber Edition, pp. 54-61. The edition prefaces this with the remark (translated from the German): "The deep tone-level at which this piece moves has given rise to the conjecture that it was originally intended for lute." If, for example, one played the Bouree to any knowledgeable musician who had never heard it before, the inevitable reaction would be "why is it written so low in pitch?" Ernest Newman's objection that "no musician could listen to a piece of music he had never heard before . . . and say that the pitch was low" is therefore ill-considered, to say the least.

If we ask what might have caused the impression of "lower pitch than usual" given to Miss Jourdain by the music she heard, there appear to be two possible kinds of answer. First, the selection of instruments in the band might have been somewhat more lowpitched in the average than what is usual today. Wanda Landowska, in her book, *Music of the Past* (1926, section on "The Color of the 18th Century Orchestra," p. 113) quotes Wagner as saying: "The application of the methods of modern instrumentation would be the surest means of rendering the theme and character of the old works unrecognisable." Miss Jourdain's impression might, on this account, have been a veridical one of instrumental quality characteristic of some actual band at Versailles in the eighteenth century, in which lower pitched instruments were more predominant than they are in bands today.

Secondly, it is well known that the absolute pitch associated with the note A used for tuning rose fairly steadily during the centuries previous to 1939 when pitch was last standardized. An A tuning fork used at the Paris Opera in 1700 was found to give a note of 404 cycles per second, which is our G approximately. Towards the end of the 18th century a piece written in C would probably have sounded to us as B, a semitone lower. If Miss Jourdain had some trace of absolute pitch, she would have recognized that the key was a strange one for that kind of music, and the natural interpretation would be that it was a piece in C sounded low pitch rather than one in B flat sounded high pitch. A deduction of this kind might be made unconsciously, being further induced perhaps by the unexpectedly less brilliant tone quality of the music.

While these explanations are of course conjectural, it seems clear that there are satisfactory explanations of the impression which Miss Jourdain recorded, on the hypothesis that it was retrocognitively veridical. At the very least the argument that Miss Jourdain's description of the music as at a pitch "lower than usual" casts doubt on the paranormal character of her experience appears baseless.

Indeed Whiteman has beaten Rollo Myers and Ernest Newman at their own game.

However, there is a much more important implication of the Versailles case which needs to be noted and that is: What relationship does this music case have to NAD? With this case of retrocognition we have shown that "psychic music" appears not only as a sole phenomenon, but that it can appear with nearly every other type of psychical phenomenon. I also said that *An Adventure* is somewhat akin to haunting phenomena (once we disregard the science fiction element of time travel)—apparitions were seen, ghostly music was heard, phantom buildings were viewed—a complete visual replay of the psychic ether! As with hauntings, the

123

music which was perceived from a distance was not strikingly elegant, but almost muted. Thus, just as hauntings may include aural perceptions, so may complex cases of retrocognition share a similar mechanical *modus operandi*.

When we view transcendental music in the light of mystical experience, it is no wonder that this phenomenon is so keenly considered a religious discipline. When we classify NAD as occurring near the point of death, and note its frequence amongst Catholic mystics and spirit mediums, and during out-of-the-body travel, it is obvious that a religious heritage is in some way connected with psychic music, as it is with most other psychic phenomena.

Transcendental music is one of the many apparently psychical manifestations noted during outbreaks of religious mania and revivals. During the Huguenot persecutions in France, toward the end of the seventeenth century, celestial music was constantly heard—including the singing of psalms by an invisible chorus.

During the great Irish Revival of 1859 and the Welsh Revival of 1904, music was heard, often accompanied by psychic lights. Similar music is recorded in the history of the Mormons who, like the Huguenots, were persecuted for many years.

Can there be any doubt that the following were in fact "religious" experiences? The intensity of the religious overtones to which the experience is prone is more fully developed in cases concerning mystics. We present four rather odd cases of particular note from Herbert Thurston's *Surprising Mystics* (Burns & Oates, 1955; Regnery Co., 1966).

Case No. 84 — Dominica ·Clara Moes

This case is rather recent. Dominica Clara Moes (1832-95) founded the Dominican Convent of Lempertsberg (Luxemburg). The case is similar not only to those of such mystics as Richard Rolle, but also to many of those described as having the experience in normal states of consciousness. This incident took place in 1877:

The storm of temptation continued unabated throughout the whole of Advent, but on Christmas Day, as she believed, a marvellous cohort of angels revealed themselves to her with *strains of heavenly music,* proclaiming the glory of the new born Savior.

Case No. 85 — Marie Julie Jahenny

Of even more recent date is the case of Marie Julie Jahenny (1850-1941) a Breton peasant and stigmatist. In this report, the phenomenon was more objective and, one might add, more medium-istic. In fact, it is vaguely similar to the reports about D. D. Home:

On 19 Sept. 1882, Dr. Imbert himself was present when M. J. announced in ecstasy that both the ring and the crown of thorns [the stigmata] would take a more elaborate form. She repeated in her trance the words she had heard from the Archangel Raphael who had promised that when the transformation occurred there would be an angelic concert and that he himself would conduct it. The prediction was verified on 24 May, 1883 and we are told that the family who alone were present were twice privileged to hear the music of the angels.

Case No. 86 — Orsola Benincasa

As the nature of the phenomena becomes more complex, the line between the "mystical" and the "mediumistic" becomes correspond-ingly less apparent. We have mentioned that certain mediums who produce various musical effects also have an affinity for the produc-tion of the "direct voice." What then of this case of "direct music" which seems to fall right into the concept of a medium? The per-cipient was Orsola Benincasa (1547-1618), who lived in Naples and founded an order of nuns later to be affiliated with the Theatines. A process of beatification was prompted in 1627 but was not fully realized, although in 1793 a decree was published praising her mys-tical bents.

At such times [in ecstasy] musical sounds, which some of the nuns described as like the song of a bird, seemed to come from her breast. They watched her lips intently but could perceive no kind of movement. She did not sing, they said, but they heard a ravishing harmony which could only have a supernatural origin. . . . Silas, Gorres, and Imbert-Gourbeyre declare that a sound came from within her breast which was like that of an organ being played.

Case No. 87 — Christina of Saint-Trond

The preceding case of Orsola Benincasa is almost precisely ante-dated and precedented by the eleventh-century mystic, Christina of Saint-Trond. Her main biography appeared eight years after her death written by Thomas de Chantimpre, O.P. Even though Herbert Thurston, an authority on these matters, considered the report "untrustworthy," we do find the following quotation which parallels similar incidents:

> She sometimes visited the nuns of the convent of St. Catherine just outside of Saint-Trond and there, it is stated, that when some pious conversation arose about Christ our Lord she would suddenly and unexpectedly be rapt by the spirit and her body would rotate whirlingly like a child's hoop, revolving so rapidly that it was impossible to distinguish the outline of her separate limbs. [This phenomenon is quite common in Catholic hagiology.] However, as the movement quieted down, "a marvellous harmony" such as no human ear had ever listened to, made itself audible, which seemed to come between her throat and her chest. There appeared to be words, but no separate words were distinguishable and no trace of breath issued from either mouth or nose.

Are these psychical phenomena or mystical phenomena? Or can there be any distinction between the two? This then brings us to the area of mediumship which we developed in an earlier chapter. It is suggested by the previous statements that these "mystical" cases involved choral music. However, with mediumship the music takes on, more often, an orchestral timbre. (There are, of course, exceptions to the rule.)

Case No. 88 — Mary Jobson

Mary Jobson was an obscure English medium who lived before the birth of organized research. Some of what we know of her comes from a tiny book entitled *A Faithful Record of the Miraculous Case of Mary Jobson* by Dr. Reid Clanny, which appeared in 1841. According to Dr. Clanny, Mary Jobson had convulsions at the age of thirteen during which "raps" manifested. This was followed by more complex incidents of telekinesis. It was during this period that she began to give accurate prophecies. Among her mediumistic phenomena were the "direct voice" and music. Witnesses to the music were her governess, Elizabeth Gauntlett, and a Dr. Drury. The latter writes: "On listening I distinctly heard most exquisite music, which continued during the time I might count a hundred. This she told me she often heard."

Case No. 89 — Salvanadin

In India, Mr. M. Jacolliot was investigating similar phenomena with the Indian medium, Salvanadin. Of one séance reported in his book *Occult Sciences in India* (Rider and Co.), he writes:

> The same fakir made one scale of a balance fall with a peacock's feather when it had a weight of 176 pounds on the opposite side. A wreath of flowers fluttered about in the air by a mere imposition of hands. *Musical sounds were heard in the air* and a shadowy hand drew luminous figures in space.

These exact phenomena were recorded with the great medium D. D. Home.

We have examined the psychical relevance of these phenomena;

127

however, we have not considered the musicological implications. Obviously we have before us a phenomenon as old as man and one which is connected with religion—for have not music, painting, and sculpture always been related to religious aesthetics, and has not religion always made use of art and music as an integral part of worship? I doubt if any musician has not, at least once, wondered: "Where does music come from?" The question is not as superficial as might be thought, for many philosophers as well as musicians have echoed this very inquiry.

Chapter 8

NAD and Its Relevancy to the Survival Issue

When I commenced work on this study, I must admit I knew virtually nothing about the phenomenon of paranormal music. Other than two case reports *in litt.*, a few references to Bozzano, the cases in Robert Crookall's books, and those in *Phantasms of the Living*, I had never given the data much thought. Further, I had no conception of where the data would lead. Such discussions as the psychic ether theory, NAD and apparition cases, NAD and the OOBE were not blueprinted or planned before the writing of these pages. They were incorporated and developed only after I had collected abundant case material; and, in fact, many of the patterns occurring in the cases were discovered during the actual drafts of the book. My only initial plan was to present the phenomena along Crookallian lines—that is, by cases quoted in toto, with points of coincidence and recurrent patterns emphasized. Since no authoritative representation of these data has previously been published (even Bozzano's discussions were scant, and translations of his treatises rare) it may fairly well be said that this volume was written without bias; though I have never hesitated to express survivalistic views on psychical phenomena when warranted.

Another admission must be made. Before embarking on this psychic adventure, I could never clearly see Bozzano's point that "celestial" music could be of advantage to proponents of the survivalistic hypothesis. In fact, I doubted that the phenomena would show intrinsic value for any theoretical viewpoint. However, as the work progressed, I found a more acute association than I had expected. I think the reader can easily ascertain from the many candid remarks scattered throughout the case material that I believe the phenomena weave directly in with the survival complex—that grand mosaic in which all parapsychological phenomena may be shown to relate to man's survival after death. (Even such theorists as Whately Carington and G. N. M. Tyrrell, both champions of the telepathic explanation of most paranormal experiences, conceded that the nature of telepathy was itself indicative of some independent agent of the human consciousness capable of surviving death.)

In order to emphasize this point, I shall devote an entire discussion to the evidence for survival from our case material.

Evidence of Survival from NAD and the
out-of-the-Body Experience

The existence of the OOBE has many relevancies to the survival issue. First, it seems to show that the consciousness may be severed from the physical organism and act independently of it for short durations during the subject's normal life. It is logical to assume that after death the consciousness may likewise exist without a dependence on the physical body. Secondly, in many OOBE's a "subtle body" is observed (which may sometimes be perceived by a second party as an apparition), which would represent the mechanical means of this survival. Various arguments may be expounded in favor of the objectivity (though supraphysical) of the double: It has been collectively perceived; the subject may see a cordal linkage between his two bodies inexplicable on any "body-image" psychological explanation; and doubles have been known to influence physical matter. (For example, Sylvan Muldoon, an habitual projector, notes his success in setting a metronome in motion during an OOBE.)

Another survivalistic element of the OOBE is those narratives of the pseudo-dead—those rather exotic cases in which persons having been pronounced dead have been restored to life—who invariably describe having, at that moment, experienced an OOBE state and *in almost every* case became convinced that they had gone through the death experience and would eventually survive it. (In Robert Crookall's *The Study and Practice of Astral Projection,* twenty-one cases of pseudo-death are cited. Twenty-five further cases are presented in the sequel *More Astral Projections.* These comprise cases 1-21 and 322-46 respectively.)

More evidence is presented by the "dead" themselves (through mediums) who have described their deaths in terms parallel to those having OOBEs and pseudo-death.

Psychic music is one of the experiences of the OOBE—this has already been pointed out in Chapter 2. The phenomenon may be likened to a particular group of OOBEs. Apart from momentary astral excursions to familiar settings, many OOBEs (more often natural than enforced) have involved a "change of environment" and have reported their OOBEs to the "other world" to which the subtle body corresponds. We have already quoted several cases in which projectors have encountered the permanently projected (Chapter 4). In Crookall's collection these represent 22.6 per cent and 16.2 per cent of 214 and 37 cases, N and EN respectively.

In this connection, we pointed out that music was heard in thirteen cases. Further, these few reports are of the "natural" classification in which a "change of environment" is more prone to occur, and are closer to the "other world." Secondly, many of our reporters did, in fact, experience a "change of environment": M. E. Henley was projected to a large room, guided by a "helper," and heard music (Case No. 2); Kathleen Snowden during her OOBE saw welcoming figures along with hearing music (Case No. 4); Doyle's correspondent saw the departed as she enjoyed a celestial concert (Case No. 12). During the fantastic ecstasy of J. W. Skelton (Case No. 13) he saw singing discarnates. All of these individuals were certain that they had momentarily entered the "other world."

Case No. 90 — W. E. Butler

W. E. Butler was an occultist whose numerous books reveal a curious mixture of psychic insight and occult fantasy, and it becomes quite difficult in cases such as these to distinguish between actual psychic occurrences and what the author "borrowed" from other accounts. Nevertheless, in his overwritten digest *The Magician, His Training and Work* (Aquarian Press, 1967), he gives an excellent account of an OOBE which most likely did occur, though its context in the book (that is, being projected by an unnamed "master") is quite fantastic. As in so many occult books, it appears to be a curious bit of storytelling modeled after a true experience. He writes:

> . . . something seemed to snap in my head [this is often mentioned—experiences ranging from "popping" to "clicking" at the time of exteriorization] and all my consciousness left me for the moment. When I again became aware of things [it appears that Butler underwent the "blackout" effect] I found myself standing by the side of the couch, looking down on some one who lay there where a short time ago I know I had been lying.

Butler saw the "cord" as a pulsating cord of bluish-gray substance. This peculiar hue of the cord had not been previously written about in the occult literature of Butler's time, but is noted in some of Crookall's writings. No point of attachment seems to be indicated in the narrative.

He goes on to say:

> I discerned glimpses of landscapes, of mountains, and lakes, and here and there faces which I had long loved since and lost awhile.

Butler heard a voice beckoning him back, but did not heed it and subsequently felt the pull of the cord:

Once again the melodies of heaven sounded around and within me, once again the vision of the light formed before me [we quoted several cases which included glowing balls of light in Chapter 2] and then with an agonizing wrench, I was back in my physical body. [Such repercussions are not generally known in occult literature other than a few references in Muldoon's writings—see Appendices. This feature was not fully realized until Crookall.]

Generally, this case, including both the "change of environment" and hearing music, has characteristics (the hue of the cord, the snapping sounds, and repercussions) that taken collectively were not known at the time Butler wrote his occult reminiscences. Compare his occult-oriented narrative to the following one:

Case No. 91 — A Young Boy

Several OOBEs have been recorded while under anesthetics. We augmented this by adding cases of NAD under the same conditions. This narrative is from an anonymous report noted in Celia Green's *Lucid Dreams,* which constitutes the Proceedings of the Institute of Psychophysical Research (Hamish Hamilton Ltd., 1967).

At the . . . age of seven years my first "out of body experience" (although I was not aware at the time) was induced by chloroform. At the moment anesthesia took over I was aware that the doctors and nurses were about to set my fractured shin and thigh . . . *sounds of music of a tone I had never heard before came to my ears,* the music was so enchanting that I left my bed [apparently in the astral body] and commenced to walk in the direction of the sound. [Note that the subject does not describe the music as being choral, which seems to be reserved for cases induced naturally.] It led me to a winding path and through a beautiful valley decked with magnificent flowers and radiant colors, the perfume of which seemed to exhilarate me, urge me on to the not-far-distant mountains. Eventually I arrived at the foot of the mountains and there I saw a white-robed figure, beckoning me onward. With hurried steps I tried to reach him, but the glorious light surrounding him seemed to fade, and in the space of seconds the scene vanished from my sight. The next thing I knew I wakened to find myself gazing at the ward ceiling.

Celia Green notes that this case contains an emotional content not associated with dreams. (And certain elements of Butler's OOBE cannot be explained away as a dream experience.)

Clearly cases such as these have survivalistic merit. Any critic wishing to discredit the music heard in these instances as hallucination will be forced to explain why music heard in natural projections is heard vividly and usually as choral, while enforced projectors usually depict it dispassionately and mainly as orchestral.

Evidence of Survival from NAD in Normal
States of Consciousness

From a general standpoint there is little direct evidence for survival from these cases. One may say that, since NAD experiences occur in the same conditions that OOBEs occur, the two phenomena are entirely interlaced.

Secondly, many identified the music as supernormal and as something quite external to their own minds or creative capabilities, even when not perceived collectively. (This is based on data collected from the questionnaire sent to each personal correspondent.)

Thirdly, many cases report the music as choral, which implies that the music was produced by humanlike voices; which could only be attributed to discarnate activity, especially when heard collectively. In this respect we have shown that the phenomenon may function on two levels—instrumental or choral—and that the choral experiences represent a more perfect form of the occurrence and its perception. Consequently, as the phenomenon becomes more perfect, it likewise becomes more humanoid. In OOBEs and death experiences, discarnates may actually be seen singing, as in Case Nos. 93, 94, and 96.

134

Case No. 92 — Edith Ventresse

Mrs. Ventresse (Devonshire, Great Britain) wrote me on November 28, 1968:

> On Christmas Eve, I think 1956, but am not sure, we had decorated the cottage throughout with holly and mistletoe as usual and went to bed about midnight, and were soon asleep. To my astonishment *I woke to hear children singing carols so sweetly near by.* I woke my husband, remarking it was surely too late for children to be abroad singing, even on Christmas Eve; the time was 1:45 a.m. My husband went to the window and looked out, the night was brilliantly starlit and silent. Still, in memory I treasure the exquisite purity of those children's voices.

Evidence of Survival from NAD Related to Death

Clearly these cases must represent the cornerstone in our argument. As pointed out, several cases have been reported at deathbeds—both by observers and the dying themselves. In most cases the music is heard as choral—and again a discarnate source is implied.

Case No. 93 — M. A. Larcombe

This case reported by Mrs. M. A. Larcombe was dated July 17, 1882, and was part of the evidence collected by the Society for Psychical Research for their work *Phantasms of the Living.*

> When I was about eighteen or nineteen, I went to stay in Guernsey. This would be about thirty years ago. About 10 a.m., one day, I was sitting in the kitchen, blowing up the fire with the bellows. I heard some very beautiful music and stopped to listen, at the same time looking up. I saw above me thousands of angels, as tight as they could be packed, seeming to rise far above and beyond me. They were only visible as far as the head and shoulders. In front

135

of them all I saw my friend, Anne Cox. As I looked and listened, *the music seemed to die away in the distance,* and at the same time, the angels seemed to pass away into the distance, and vanish like smoke.

I ran up to Miss White, the young lady staying in the house, and told her what I had seen. She said, "You may be sure your friend, Anne Cox, has gone to Heaven." I wrote home at once, to Lyme Regis, and found that Anne Cox had died that very day. Anne Cox and I had been very close friends. She was just my own age and was almost like a sister to me.

Mrs. Larcombe states positively that she was in no anxiety about her friend and had no knowledge of her illness. She has had no other hallucinations, unless an unexplained appearance seen by her in early childhood, and by others as well as herself, was of that character.

The authors of *Phantasms* also added that she is a "sensible and superior person who has seen a good deal of the world."

We theorize that the death experience brings us closer to the "other world" than in any other state, and that its properties may be momentarily perceived by the living. I would challenge any anti-survivalist to explain the phenomenon if man did not survive death. Certain implications emphasizing the survival hypothesis are realized in cases where music is heard and apparitions are seen.

Case No. 94 — Fred —

The following letter was sent to me by Mrs. F. Downing of North Ipswich, Great Britain on December 28, 1968:

My brother Fred, who has recently passed on, after serious illness, had this experience [of hearing music] whilst in the hospital and one month previous to his passing. Fred was deeply unconscious for three days and no one expected he would regain consciousness. However he did, but he was never told of being in that state. When he was able to talk . . . he spoke about the music and the children. It seemed to have made a big impression upon him as he kept repeating, "So many children, so much music," he smiled, "and so much noise." [Astral projectors talk of deafening roaring sounds.]

Usually the voices are said to have been female; rarely are they male—cases involving children's voices seem to be of the former group.

Myers pointed out in his *Human Personality and Its Survival of Bodily Death* that music cases heard related to death show a direct manifestation of personality. In several of our cases, music was heard in relation to the deaths of musicians or persons passionately fond of music. Myers seemed to imply, as we have developed, that the NAD is usually heard under the same conditions that an apparition might be expected to appear. And again, music and apparitions have been perceived simultaneously (for example, Case Nos. 38, 45, 94).

There is one point of evidence that will be presented here—that, just as the "dead" describe (through mediums) OOBEs at the moment of death, the "dead" have also described having heard music at their passing exactly as have the dying. Compare Case Nos. 95 and 96 with No. 97.

Case No. 95 — Arthur Hill

Mrs. Edith Ventresse wrote on November 28, 1968:

My father, Arthur James Hill of Roadwater Farm, Washford, Somerset, as he lay dying on July 18, 1939, asked my mother and me, "Where is the music coming from?" Hearing nothing, we suggested it was our neighbor's radio. With a smile of great sweetness and wisdom he shook his head and said, "No, it isn't that." This was perhaps at 10:00 a.m., and he ceased to breathe about 5:00 p.m."

137

Case No. 96 — "Sissy"

The second case of this type was originally published in *Light* (April, 1900) and was narrated by Dr. Paul Edwards:

While living in a country town in California about the year 1887, I was called upon to visit a very dear lady friend who was very low and weak from consumption. Everyone knew that this pure and noble wife and mother was doomed to die, and at last she herself became convinced that immediate death was inevitable, and accordingly she prepared for the event. Calling her children to her bedside she kissed each in turn, sending them away as soon as goodbye was said. Then came the husband's turn to step up and bid farewell to a most loving wife, who was perfectly clear in her mind. She began by saying "........, do not weep over me, for I am without pain and am wholly serene. I love you upon earth, and shall love you after I have gone. I am fully resolved to come to you if such a thing is possible, and if it is not possible I will be waiting when you all come. My first desire now is to go. . . . I see people moving —all in white. *The music is strangely enchanting*—Oh! here is Sadie; she is with me—and—she knows who I am." (Sadie was a little girl she had lost about ten years before.) "Sissy!" said the husband, "you are out of your mind." "Oh dear! Why did you call me here again?" said the wife. "Now it will be hard for me to go away again; I was so pleased while there—it was so delightful—so soothing." In about three minutes the dying woman added: "I am going away again and will not come back to you even if you call me."

This scene lasted for about eight minutes, and it was very plain that the dying wife was in full view of the two worlds at the same time, for she described how the moving figures looked in the world beyond, as she directed her words to mortals in this world.

I think that of all my death scenes this was the most impressive—the most solemn.

138

Case No. 97 — A "Communicator"

This interesting account is taken from Gertrude O. Tubby's excellent, though extremely rare, book *James H. Hyslop—X, His Book* (York Printing Co., 1928). As students of parapsychological history are aware, Tubby was Hyslop's assistant. During his researches Hyslop had instituted experiments in cross-references—experiments whereby specific "communicators" would give evidence of their survival by concordant or complementary messages through different mediums. After Hyslop's death, Tubby received evidential communications from the Hyslop-persona in this precise manner. These records comprise the volume.

During these experiments many contacts were received from other communicators. In a sitting with an obscure American sensitive, Mrs. Louise M. Chamberlaine, the following was recorded. The speaker is the medium's control relaying the message from a "communicator." The parenthetical words are those of Tubby.

From a sitting October 6, 1924, Séance No. 12:

Now did she have an attack of grippe the winter before she died and was very sleepless? (yes.)
And during that time she seemed to have thought she heard singing. (I see.) Now she says she was not mistaken. (Good, who was it singing?)
She heard singing from the other world, and she now knows about it.

Unfortunately here the narrative ends. The survivalist implication is clear—the "dead" report experiences the dying are known to have had.

Evidence of Survival from NAD and Hauntings

After briefly surveying the various theories of haunting phenomena, it was decided that survivalistically oriented theories cover the wide range of manifestations more easily than telepathic or psycho-

139

metric theories. In certain hauntings, which may be shown to be of a spiritistic nature, music was perceived, as in the following cases.

Case No. 98 — David Hunter

This case was reported in Andrew Lang's *Cock Lane and Common Sense* (Longmans, Green & Co., Ltd., 1894):

> David Hunter, "neat-herd at the house of the Bishop of Down and Connor, at Portmore, in 1663" was haunted by the ghost of an elderly woman who was disturbed about a debt of twenty-eight shillings which had not been paid. Mr. Hunter did not even know the ghost when she was alive; but she made herself so much at home in his dwelling that "his little dog would follow her as well as his master." The ghost, however, was invisible to Mrs. Hunter. When Hunter had at last executed her commission she asked him to lift her up in his arms. She "felt just like a bag of feathers; so she vanished and *he heard most delicate music* as she went off over his head." Sceptics attributed the phenomena to *potheen*,[1] but how could *potheen* tell Hunter about the ghost's debt and reveal that the money to discharge it was hidden under her hearthstone?

Case No. 99 — Borley's Church

A fairly representative case of a purely musical haunting is that of Borley's Church (not to be confused with Borley Rectory, which was across from it). Harry Price, whose investigation of Borley Rectory has been thrown into question,[2] nevertheless compiled evidence worthy of serious consideration that Borley's Church was also

---

[1] Potheen is illegal home-brewed Irish whiskey.

[2] The original records were published in Price's *The Most Haunted House in England*. Criticisms of the case were published in an S. P. R. *Proceedings* by Trevor H. Hall, Eric J. Dingwall, and K. M. Goldney. Hall's wild accusations about other prominent parapsychologists have now discredited him. Mrs. Goldney has since changed her conviction of

haunted. The records are in one of Price's last books, *The End of Borley Rectory* (Harrap & Co. Ltd., 1946). Price reports that "even during my tenancy of the Rectory, it was reported to me that 'music and choir-singing' had been heard in Borley Church at night, when it was certain that the church was locked and empty." The combination of human voices and organ has been encountered in other cases throughout this volume.

Later in his book Price cites additional evidence for these musical effects:

> Another possible audible clue is the choir-singing and organ music which a number of villagers declare have been heard in the building containing neither worshipers nor choristers and was securely locked. We have firsthand evidence. Mr. Hardy, Junior, happening to pass the church at night, heard singing or chanting coming from the fabric which was in complete darkness, empty and locked.

Accordingly, as with the OOBE, while not in itself clearly survivalistic, psychic music is found working within a decidedly survivalistic framework. Our own theory of hauntings, a revision of the psychic ether theory, which was especially formulated to include music phenomena, presupposes survival after death. Most of the references we cited concern cases whose most notable distinctions were spiritistic—phantoms, evidence of purpose, and the like.

---

the truth of the criticism, which went so far as to accuse Price of faking his results of the haunting, and has now stated that she considers the conclusions of Hall and Dingwall as "doubtful." (See, e.g., *Journal* S. P. R., Volume 39, No. 697, pages 303-6). The historian W. H. Salter (*Zoar*) has expressed his view in a milder form—that Price distorted testimony. However, since it has become *fashionable* to accuse both parapsychologists and their subjects of being fraudulent, and since these meek exposures never seem to explain even half of the phenomena, they will not concern us. The S. P. R. has now published a lengthy report by Robert J. Hastings vindicating Price and throwing new light on both the criticisms and the critics (*Proceedings* S.P.R. Volume 55, part 201).

One such case presented next was originally part of the case material collected for *Phantasms of the Living*. It is a very odd case —one which could have been placed in several of our categories but is, I think, a good example of a collectively perceived haunting which was perceived in a different manner by each of the percipients.

Case No. 100 — Lady C. and Miss Z. T.

October 13, 1884

In October, 1879, I was staying at Bishopthorpe, near York, with the Archbishop of York. I was sleeping with Miss Z. T. when I suddenly saw a white figure fly through the room from the door to the window. It was only a shadowy form and passed in a moment. I felt utterly terrified and called out at once, "Did you see that?" and at the same moment Miss Z. T. exclaimed, "Did you hear that?" Then I said instantly, "I saw an angel fly through the room," and she said, "I heard an angel singing." We were both very much frightened for a little while, but said nothing about it to any one.

Miss Z. T.'s confirming account was written two months later. It substantially agrees with the account of Lady C.:

December 19, 1884

Late one night, about October 17, 1879, Lady C. (then Lady K. L.) and I were preparing to go to sleep, after talking some time, when I heard something like very faint music and seemed to feel what people call "a presence." I put out my hand and touched Lady C. saying, "Did you hear that?" She said, "Oh don't! Just now I saw something going across the room!" We were both a good deal frightened, and tried to go to sleep as soon as we could. But I remember asking Lady C. exactly what she had seen, and she said, "A sort of white shadow, like a spirit." The above occurred at Bishopthorpe, York.

142

Evidence of Survival from Mystics and Mediums

Most of this data is self-explanatory. Mystics and mediums represent persons who produce phenomena which, apart from NAD, are oriented toward survival. Specific cases of mediumship whose productions are hardly explainable by anything other than survival—Home and Moses—also produced music. In fact, of the mediums mentioned in Chapter 6, three were "direct-voice" mediums (Blake, Margery, and Home on rare occasions) which is probably the most spiritistic genre of all.

It should be brought out that both Roman Catholic saints and mediums have also reported OOBEs. In Roman Catholic lore the phenomenon is known as bi-location. Specific cases of astral projection are recorded in the lives of Saint Anthony of Padua, Saint Severus of Ravenna, Saint Ambrose, Saint Clement of Rome, and Alphonse de Liguori. On the other hand OOBE cases are rich within mediumistic biographies. As a gentle sampling, specific reports of OOBEs may be found in the case of Mrs. Piper, who claimed that "helpers" took her out of her body while she slept, and she noted seeing the "silver cord" extension. She also mentioned the cord extension when leaving her trance on one occasion. Mrs. Leonard and Mrs. Garrett have described spontaneous cases. Both D. D. Home and W. Stainton Moses describe being taken out of their bodies by discarnates. Franek Kluski, the Polish physical medium, described such experiences in his youth. Stephen Ossowieski, who although known as a clairvoyant was also a physical medium, claimed the ability to externalize his double. And both the early English medium J. J. Morse and the contemporary Danish physical medium Einar Nielsen described OOBEs on entering trance. Comments suggestive of the OOBE have been made by Mrs. Willett (who talked about "walking out of yourself"), Eusapia Palladino (who often saw her own double), and the voice mediums Margery and Centurione Scotto (both of whom described the experience of falling through a deep hole [the tunnel effect]).

In these data, we again come across the relationship between OOBEs and celestial music.

Apart from the experiences of the dying, mediumistic communications have struck upon the "music of the spheres," thus completing the case for evidence of survival.

From another perspective, traditionally both occidental and oriental mystics have referred to the NAD as not only supraphysical, but as a property of the "other-world." This feature is clear in the musical heaven of the Tantric Buddhists. Roman Catholic thought has a similar approach to the phenomenon.

Case No. 101 — John Milton

The notion that discarnates produce astral music is hit upon by no less a remarkable source than Montague Summers (*Witchcraft and Black Magic*, Rider & Co., 1958). Summers also spoke from a more or less traditional Roman Catholic viewpoint. In reference to some lines of the great English poet John Milton, who apparently heard a celestial choir, he states of the NAD, ". . . these are holy invocations and vocal aspirations, and the celestial music of masses and litanies, echoes caught from the choristers of Paradise, having the Harps of God such music as Milton heard." Tantric Yoga holds the same view, that earthly music is but an echo of the "audible life stream." The lines from Milton upon which Summers comments read:

> There let the pealing Organ blow
> To the full voic'd Quire below
> In Service high and Anthems clear
> As may with sweetness, through mine ear
> Dissolve me into ecstasies
> And bring all Heaven before mine eyes.

It therefore should not be startling to note that W. H. Salter, one of the foremost historians of psychical research, notes in his book

144

on survival evidence, *Zoar*, that Milton in another poem describes an experience similar to an OOBE.

The critical point to be observed is that Summers, in his remarks, implies a discarnate source of the music; and apparently the Roman Catholic viewpoint on the phenomenon is antiquated, judging from his statements. It may be concluded from this that psychic music is no cultural artifact of the modern psychic movement, but has deep-seated origins.

We can categorize the direct and implied survivalistic content of the phenomenon in a set of clear-cut statements:

1. Persons hearing the NAD in normal states of consciousness have felt the music to be beyond their own imagination and creative aptitude, and to be caused by some external agent. Rarely have incarnate (for example, telepathic) sources been found.

2. A great many cases occur during OOBEs which constitute a momentary death experience. The music was heard most vividly as human voices and seemed to issue from the "other world" during "change of environment" OOBEs.

3. The dying have heard celestial music and nearly always attribute it to a discarnate source. Cases are reported where music and apparitions have been seen and heard simultaneously.[3] Cases related to death were perceived in much the same way as an apparition and show evidence of personality and purpose.

4. The "dead" themselves tell of having heard music at their own deaths, and they report the existence of music in the "other world."

5. Music has been heard during spiritistic manifestations — in hauntings and mediumistic séances.

6. Both Roman Catholic and Tantric Buddhist thought, as well as modern spiritistic concepts, have always regarded the phenomenon as a property of the "other world."

---

[3] According to the Hindu Shastras, the yogi, after hearing "celestial voices and songs" will witness the etherealization of apparitional forms.

A prolonged discussion of the survivalistic elements of the phenomenon can not be given adequate representation. I have only presented a few empirical arguments which, in summary form, seem to indicate survival. Happily, from my standpoint, so little has been written about the phenomenon that there are no strong countertheories to my own to debate—except perhaps, René Sudre's rash theory of "pathological hallucinations," which I think needs little comment. The existence of collective cases immediately voids his conclusion.

Actually such a discussion should be unnecessary. I would hope that the survivalistic impact of the data would strike the reader as forcibly as it did this author.

As I stated at the beginning of the volume, the deep problem of man's survival of death, to which Bozzano's argumentation was directed, is not the primary concern of this manuscript. The strategy of this short digest is to present enough case material to reinstate celestial music as a phenomenon worthy of parapsychology's concern. It is often the case that in presenting such data a writer gets caught up in the wonderland (or should I say labyrinth) of psychical phenomena, so that short argumentary excursions into other realms of consideration are forthcoming at varying intervals. We need not give lengthy theoretical dissertations on the *a priori* evidences of survival from "other-world" experiences. This has already been formidably done by such eminent parapsychologists as Drs. Crookall, Hart, and Whiteman.

I can only hope that I have done justice to an immense but forgotten phenomenon.

Postscript
by Robert Crookall
B.Sc. (Psychology), D.Sc., Ph.D.

Transcendental, or supernormal, music receives its first critical appraisal in this interesting book, and the job has been well worth undertaking.

The first question considered is whether phenomena of this remarkable type actually occur—whether they are genuine phenomena. The author cites a considerable body of evidence in support of this claim: While some people may imagine that they hear nonphysical music, there is good reason to conclude that others have heard "music" that was by no means merely imagined.

If the phenomena occurred solely in connection with death, we would be justified in strongly suspecting that they were merely subjective and private to the individual experiences, that they were hallucinations. But Mr. Rogo shows that they also occur with quite normal people who are nowhere near death, a notable case being that of Raymond Bayless, the well-known parapsychologist (who, indeed, first drew Mr. Rogo's attention to these intriguing matters). Bayless's experience of "celestial" music, cited in the book, speaks for itself as a good example of the "music of the spheres." Similar phenomena, it is pointed out, are well known among Roman Catholic "saints," as was shown by Father H. Thurston, S.J.

Mr. Rogo devotes a whole chapter (Chapter 3) to normal cases. He found that they can be subdivided into two groups: (1) those in which the "music" heard was of the vocal kind and (2) those in which it was nonvocal, and he is able to make a significant correlation—(1) people who "hear" vocal music are of the nonmediumistic bodily constitution, that is, the bulk of people, while (2) people

147

who "hear" nonvocal music are of the mediumistic constitution, that is, with a somewhat loose, fluid, extensible, and projectable vehicle of vitality (the "vital body" of the Rosicrucians, the "Bardo Body" of the Tibetans, the "etheric double" of the Theosophists, etc.). Thus, (1) the released doubles of those who hear vocal music consist of the "superphysical" Soul Body only (the Desire Body of the Rosicrucians, the Emotional Body of the Theosophists, the Body of Light of the Tibetans, etc.), while (2) the doubles of those who hear nonvocal music include not only the Soul Body but also part of the "semiphysical" vehicle of vitality. Again, (1) those who hear vocal music tend to hear crescendos and diminuendos, while (2) those who hear nonvocal music tend to hear sudden bursts of music. Mr. Rogo therefore correlates the fact that transcendental music is heard with out-of-the-body experiences, and he correlates the different kinds of music heard with different kinds of doubles released and, further, correlates the latter with different kinds of people, namely, mediumistic and nonmediumistic in total bodily constitution.

The celestial music heard by people who are in course of transition is shown to grade into the normal type just mentioned, as indeed might be expected, since death is merely a complete, and consequently an irreversible, evacuation of the body (in which the whole of the vehicle of vitality is projected) while, as already said, temporary out-of-the-body experiences include those of mediumistic men (with part of the vehicle of vitality projected) and those of nonmediumistic men (with none of that "semiphysical" feature projected).

There is, Mr. Rogo points out, another gradation which is highly significant: The above-mentioned cases grade into others which involve "haunted" houses. The impact on the hypothesis of survival is given due consideration: It is, indeed, most striking.

This book is a compact, well-reasoned study, based on well-authenticated cases (so far as authentication is possible), which establishes the reality of the phenomena considered, and which draws up valuable correlations among a large number of apparently distinct phenomena.

Appendix A

The Supreme Adventure: The Journey into Death

In 1961, under the auspices of the Churches' Fellowship for Psychical Study, Dr. Robert Crookall's *The Supreme Adventure* was published.[1] The volume is unique in that the psychic hypothesis of the survival after death is used as a presupposition. Based on communications sporadically received through a number of mediums, the volume analyzes the total death experience—from the moment of death to the first attempts at "communication." Analyzing the data received through over one hundred independent sensitives, striking inner corroboration of certain death episodes was enunciated: In almost every case, the "communicators" described the same recurring experiences of death. *The Supreme Adventure,* as well as Dr. Crookall's other studies, leans heavily on doctrine of the astral body, a phenomenon upon which Dr. Crookall is perhaps the greatest occidental scholar.

However, when Dr. Crookall's recent study, *Events on the Threshold of the After Life,* was issued,[2] a note of criticism called into question the "descriptive technique" therein employed.

---

[1] All references to this study will be made by the initials "Cr" and the page number.

[2] Crookall, Robert: *Events on the Threshold of the After Life* (Darshana International, Moradabad, 1967).

Peter Maddeley, in his review, stated:[3]

> But failing the instrumental detection of subtle bodies
> . . . it is hard to see how their existence can possibly even
> begin to be established by the experiences of clairvoyants,
> astral travellers, and so forth, unless it can be shown that
> the forms of such experiences are similar in a wide variety
> of cultures.

This general criticism could well be leveled at *The Supreme Adventure*, and is well deserving of being answered. Or has it already so been?

While I described the format of Dr. Crookall's volume as "unique," it is nonetheless predated by many centuries. For in the Tantric Buddhist Scripture, the *Bardo Thodol*, loosely translated as the *Tibetan Book of the Dead*, the Tibetan scholars had embarked on a similar endeavor.[4] Richly enamored of the science of death, the Buddhists who compiled the *Bardo Thodol* sought to present a script minutely detailing each experience of death. Logically, we should expect that the *Bardo Thodol* would coincide with the experiences compiled by Dr. Crookall.

The Vehicle

If man is to survive death, he should be endowed with some form of "subtle body." I have in a previous study,[5] pointed out the relationship between occidental and Tibetan doctrines of the phenomenon called "astral projection."

---

[3]Maddeley, Peter: Review of *Events on the Threshold of the After Life, Journal* S. P. R., Vol. 44, No. 735, pp. 259-60.

[4] Various editions of W. Y. Evans-Wentz's *Tibetan Book of the Dead* have been issued since its initial publication in 1927. This paper will use as reference the Oxford University Press 1960 edition. All references will be identified by the initials E-W and the page number.

[5] Rogo, D. Scott: "Astral Projection in Tibetan Buddhist Literature," *Inter. Jour. of Parapsychology*, Vol. X., No. 3.

Specifically, the *Bardo Thodol* states of the post-mortem vehicle:

> While on the second stage of the Bardo [after-death state] one's body is of the nature of that called the shining illusory body [E-W 100].

In another section, this vehicle is described as the "radiant body" (E-W 156).

These odd semantics regarding the "radiance" of the post-mortem vehicle become clearer when we relate them to the experiences of "communicators." For instance, one "communicator" cited by Crookall states, "I light dark places now where I go where it is dark. I don't know how I do it, but I seem to have a light in me which I didn't know I had before. . . . I love to go in the dark and see me shine like a candle all bright" (Anonymous, *Letters from Lancelot,* Dunstan and Co., Ltd., 1931) (Cr 132). In other words, this "communicator" noted the luminosity, the "radiance," of the astral body.

Immediately after Death

Dr. Crookall has aptly pointed out in *The Supreme Adventure* that, to "communicators," the exact experience at the moment of death is similar to astral projection. Dead relatives are often seen by the dying or nearly dead percipient; and the percipient at first may not realize that he is dead.

Several "communicators" have recounted these experiences thus:

> I saw about me those that had been dead for a long time. . . . Then I seemed to rise out of my body and come down quietly on the floor. . . . There seemed to be two of me, one on the bed and one beside the bed. [——, *Letters from Lancelot*].
>
> Then I saw that I was not lying on the bed, but floating in the air a little above it. . . . I saw my relatives still in earth-life. I spoke to them. They took no notice. [Helen Alex Dallas, *Human Survival and Its Implications,* L.S.A. Publications, Ltd., 1930].

151

Dr. Crookall has cited several other examples. And so have the Tibetan scholars. We read in the *Bardo Thodol*:

> When the consciousness-principle getteth outside (the body it sayeth to itself) . . . it seeth its relatives and connections as it had been used to seeing before [E-W 98]. . . . Although he can see them . . . they cannot hear him calling upon them so he goeth away displeased [E-W 102].

The *Bardo Thodol* also mentions the dead seeing deceased relatives.

A Review of the Past Life

Dr. Crookall has pointed out several instances in which the traveler of death experiences a panoramic review of the just-extinguished earth life (Cr 12-13). The discarnate "Myers" through the automatist Geraldine Cummins states, "I seemed to be . . . seeing pictures of my past life" (*Beyond Human Personality*, Nichelson & Watson, Ltd., 1935). A "communicator" to Jane Sherwood (*The Psychic Bridge*, Rider & Co.) states that his mind "raced over the record of a whole long lifetime." A discarnate in conversation with J. Arthur Findlay (*Where Two Worlds Meet*, Psychic Press, 1951) instructed him, "The scenes of the past life are . . . often revealed to those who are just passing, at the last moment."

The *Bardo Thodol's* student, Evans-Wentz, paraphrases a similar passage written in the ancient wisdom of that Buddhist Scripture:

> What he has thought and what he has done become objective: thought-forms having been consciously visualized and allowed to take root and grow and blossom and produce, now pass in a solemn and mighty panorama, and the consciousness-content of his personality [E-W 29].

The Sleep

One experience, not easily explained away as the product of archetypal thinking, is that, according to the "dead," and also various "occult" schools, it takes approximately three or four days for the astral body to be completely released from the corpse (the shedding of the "fluidic body" or, as Dr. Crookall terms it, the "vehicle of vitality," the shell that envelops the astral body). In that connection, for three or four days, the newly dead enter a sleep state (Cr 33-37).

"Communicators" have instructed us:

> In some cases the spirit sleeps for a week or more, if the last illness has been of an exhausting nature, or perhaps only for three days . . . [Mrs. A. L. Fernie, *Not Silent, If Dead* (Fernie, 1890)].

> I hear that some people have a deep and long sleep, that may be so—I think it must be [C. Drayton Thomas, *The Dawn beyond Death* (Lectures Universal)].

> During the three days of sleep which usually follow transition . . . [Carl Wickland, *The Gateway of Understanding* (Psychic Book Club)].

So says the *Bardo Thodol*:

> In various Tantras it is said that this state of swoon endureth for about three and one-half days. Most other (religious treatises) say for four days [E-W 93].

> Oh nobly born, thou hast been in a swoon during the last three and one-half days [E-W 105].

It has also been pointed out that the recently dead may not at first realize their own post-mortem state. "Raymond," communicating through Mrs. Leonard to Sir Oliver Lodge, has pointed out that some "don't believe that they have passed on" (*Raymond*, Doran Co.). Another "communicator" corroborates "Raymond" that some "awake at once, and in great confusion of mind as to what has happened" (F. Heslop, *Life Worth Living* [Charles Taylor]).

The Tibetan sages were apparently well aware of this post-mortem confusion. We read in the *Bardo Thodol*, "When the con-

153

sciousness-principle getteth outside [the body], it sayeth to itself 'Am I dead, or am I not dead?' It cannot determine" [E-W 98]. And later, "Not knowing whether [he be] dead or not [a state of] lucidity cometh" (E-W 100).

The Initial Post-mortem State

Dr. Crookall shows that it is not rare that the newly dead find themselves enveloped in a thick, misty environment ("Hades" condition) corresponding to the subtle "vehicle of vitality." "Myers" speaks of this as the "Plane of Illusion," according to Cummins in *Beyond Human Personality.* One clairvoyant has pictured the conditions (Sadhu Singh, *Visions of the Spiritual World* [Macmillan Co., 1925]): ". . . They [some spirits] have to remain for a considerable period in the lower and darker planes of the intermediate state." Similarly one occidental writer reports that, during the three days the "vehicle of vitality" is still connected to the physical and astral bodies, "We wander in the mists of unreality in a dreamy, half-way state (Roy Dixon-Smith, *New Light on Survival* [Rider & Co., 1952])." Robert Crookall has analyzed this "Land of Mists" extensively (Cr 14-32).

And the *Bardo Thodol* continually warns the dead from this state, describing it as "a dull, smoke-colored light from Hell" (E-W 109). This exact description is repeated a number of times in the Tibetan text.

The Final Experiences

According to various "communicators," the "dead," after perhaps wandering for a short duration, are then guided by "deliverers," other discarnates, into the light, "paradise" conditions: the glorious heavenly afterworld.

> Next came the recognition of my friends in spirit. Soon I came into full consciousness of my immediate surroundings (F. W. Fitzsimmons, *Opening the Psychic Door* [Hutchinson & Co., 1933]).

154

When I awoke completely I felt so refreshed. . . . I knew I was not on earth, not only because of the long-lost friends around me but because of the brilliancy of the atmosphere [C. Drayton Thomas, *ibid.*].

I felt a strange sort of feeling as if I were waking from a deep sleep and at first I did not know where I was. . . . After awhile, I became more fully awake and saw my wife. . . . She told me I had died. . . . Gradually I became more alive as if my faculties had just recovered from being numb. It was a pleasant sensation. [*Light*, Volume XLVII, 1927].

Similar experiences are recorded in the *Bardo Thodol*. That text states that, if one be obscured in the "dull, smoke-colored light from Hell," on the third day, "Ghagavan Ratna-Sambhava and his accompanying deities, along with the *light-path from the human world*, will come to receive one simultaneously" (E-W 110).

Of the "Paradise" condition, "communicators" have consistently described it as in this passage, "I saw running brooks, lakes, trees, grass and flowers" (Edward Randall, *The Dead Have Never Died* [Allen & Unwin Co., 1918]). Again, Dr. Crookall cites several similar extracts.

Many hundreds of years earlier the authors of the *Bardo Thodol* wrote, "As a sign [of Paradise] the sky will be cloudless, they will merge into rainbow radiance; there will be sun-showers, sweet scent of incense, *music in the skies* . . ." (E-W 135).

Activities of the Living

Based on these alleged post-mortem communications, Dr. Crookall has maintained in *The Supreme Adventure*, "Many communicators complain that the excessive grief of still-embodied friends depresses and hurts the newly dead" (Cr 64). This, of course, is again based on occidental literature and, for the main part, spiritualist literature. The point, however, is well enunciated in the *Bardo Thodol* also, wherein we read that the "spirit" "hearing the wails of grief of his relatives is depressed and angered" (E-W 102).

Expounding on this deduction, Crookall has also written, "The newly dead greatly benefit by the prayers of 'living friends'" (Cr 64). In another formidable study, *During Sleep* (London, Theosophical Publishing House, 1964), Crookall cites pages of examples of passages in spiritualist literature to that effect.

The Tibetan text, in examining this precise point, urges, "Thy living relatives may—by way of dedication for the benefits of the deceased—be sacrificing animals and performing religious ceremonies, and giving alms" (E-W 169).

I think the readers will see that Mr. Maddeley's criticism of Dr. Crookall's work has been countered; that is, his points have been amply answered by placing our psychic knowledge of all cultures into proper coincidence.

It is also noteworthy that this study has been written with only two references at hand, Dr. Robert Crookall's *The Supreme Adventure* and the Evans-Wentz edition of the *Tibetan Book of the Dead*. All spiritistic references were issued in the former, all Tibetan references in the latter. This, I feel, demonstrates the formidability of both works.

Unfortunately, in attempting to itemize the experience of death, I have been forced to violate the continuity of both Dr. Crookall's book and the Tantric text. Actually, the congruity between the two texts presents a case much stronger than can be lightly stressed in these too-brief pages.

It appears to me that Hamlet was quite incorrect when he soliloquized death as "the undiscover'd country, from whose bourn no traveller returns."

In reading this essay, one may forget that, unlike the Tibetan Scriptures, *The Supreme Adventure* is, above all, a parapsychological treatise; and that its author's knowledge in his field is unsurpassed. In reading, rereading, and studying the writings of Robert Crookall, one must ponder: Has parapsychology not answered the very questions it is saving for the future? I am thinking positively in relation to the survival hypothesis, and I think the outcome is delightfully optimistic.

Appendix B

A Survey of Literature on the out-of-the-Body Experience

Parapsychology, as with most studies, has its fads and fancies. This is no better exemplified than in the attitude given it by the general lay community—and in the last few years, as parapsychology has become more familiar to the general public, this study has seen focal points of interest centering from psychic surgery to Cayce cults. Lately, however, this interest has begun to focus on "astral projection," known also by such nomenclature as "out-of-the-body experience," "ecsomatic phenomena," and "ESP-projection." [1]

Such "fads" present a problem to both researcher and lay individual—for out-of-the-body travel literature, having such a vast amount of historical as well as current presentations, brings us to a point promulgated by Allan Angoff at the Parapsychology and Religion Conference sponsored by the Parapsychology Foundation.[2]

Allan Angoff stated that the student of parapsychology will have the dolorous task of surveying the literature of a field which, as of yet, has no clear or definitive survey or index.[3]

On this same level the literature of out-of-the-body travel presents a similar difficulty. The public having a newly engendered interest in this particular phenomenon will naturally come to recognized parapsychologists for the exact synthesis for which Mr. Angoff has enunciated the need. And since only recently, thanks to the epoch-making work of such pioneers as Professor Hornell Hart and Dr. Robert Crookall, this peculiar phenomenon has risen above the natural stigma of being labeled part of the "occult" or "arcane,"

---

[1] In discussing works in the body of this chapter, I will employ the term favored by the author whose work I am representing.

[2] A partial *Proceedings* of this conference held in 1965 may be read in the *International Journal of Parapsychology*, Vol. VIII, No. 2.

[3] Angoff, Allan: "The Literature of Religion and Parapsychology," *International Journal of Parapsychology*, Vol. VIII, No. 2.

many parapsychologists have not had the opportunity to familiarize themselves with the literature of this subject to the same extent as they have had with, for example, quantitative methods of research, general history of the field, or the literature of parapsychology and its bearing on related fields of science.

It is with this in mind that this Appendix is written—to be a somewhat comprehensive (though by no means exhaustive) annotated bibliography reviewing the more important works having a bearing on out-of-the-body phenomena.

Obviously, categorization of the various literary genres presents certain irregularities. Thus this study has not attempted to force all the literature into a limited outline framework such as by nationality, culture, or chronology, but will present the literature in self-contained categories with cross-references where necessary.

General Surveys

The first category we must approach is that of collected case material; and no better source may be found than two volumes by Dr. Robert Crookall, whose work in the field of out-of-the-body experiences is the most pioneering, authoritative, and prolific in contemporary literature. (Dr. Crookall's other works will be discussed in another category.)

The first of these volumes (*The Study and Practice of Astral Projection*, Aquarian Press, 1961; reprint, University Books Inc., 1966) presents one hundred and sixty cases of the experience categorized as "natural" (near death, ill, exhausted, or in a normal state) and "enforced" (cases induced by anesthetics, suffocation, falling, or hypnosis). A fairly complete history of the subject is given as a fifteen-page appendix with additional references to postmortem communications bearing on astral projection, sleep, and so on.

The book's complement and a far more important work is Crookall's *More Astral Projections* (Aquarian Press, London, 1964) whose main feature is two hundred and twenty-two further case studies. Many of these are drawn from preexisting sources, but there are several (and more important) firsthand accounts sent to the author. In the later volume Crookall presents in exquisite form the "pattern recurrence" technique—that all the various accounts, while in some degree deviating from each other, generally are intercorroborative; and that certain patterns in the experiences are usually recurring. On page 146 Crookall presents his most powerful discovery: that natural projections have substantially different characteristics than do enforced projections.

Celia Green's recently released *Out-of-the-Body Experiences* (Institute of Psychophysical Research, 1968) is impressive from the standpoint of sheer mass, but it offers no comprehensive study of the phenomenon.

A more "popular" book, but one of high critical value, despite sections of literary obscurity, is Susy Smith's *The Enigma of out of Body Travel*, (Helix Press, 1965). This study, more stylized than Crookall's, is a presentation of the lore of out-of-the-body experience and its various implications. These include spontaneous cases; the data of "habitual travelers" (the literature of which we shall discuss in a later section); the "chemistry" of the experience; "traveling clairvoyance," a form of the "out-of-the-body" experience in which, though the consciousness seems liberated, no other-world body is perceived; historical cases; bilocation, in which the projection vehicle is perceived by a percipient as an apparition; the experiences of mediums; cases in primitive society; ecstasy; and philosophical lore. This comprehensive volume, while a bit confusing to the novice because of considerable interchange of nomenclature, is nonetheless laudable; and favorable reviews of it may be found written by Dr. Robert Crookall (*International Journal of Parapsychology*, Volume VIII, Number 3) and Professor Hornell Hart (*Journal* A.S.P.R., Volume 60, Number 4).

A book with a quite similar format is Ralph Shirley's 1938 classic, *The Mystery of the Human Double*, now reissued in a new edition (University Books Inc., 1965). The book's feature value is twofold. First, it presents some rather obscure cases originally printed in various periodicals of its time which are inaccessible to us today (for example, *The Occult Review*). Secondly, for those not wishing to study the original sources, it provides a digest of essays on those rare individuals we term "habitual projectors." It also provides some material on hypnosis and the "double" which is better enunciated here than in Miss Smith's book, and some interesting "occult" studies usually ignored by contemporary scholars.

Not so easily accessible as the previously mentioned volumes is Sylvan Muldoon's *The Case for Astral Projection* (Aries Press, 1946). While Muldoon himself is a habitual projector, he bypasses his own experiences to a great extent, and presents other cases, both from preexisting sources and those received by the author, with his own autobiographical annotations.

Habitual Projection Literature

Another category of study is the autobiographical works of those "psychics" who have had the fortune to produce the out-of-the-body experience if not at will, at least repeatedly.

Chronologically the first major works of this nature were two long essays by Oliver Fox (pseudonym) which first appeared in the *Occult Review,* but which were published in book form in 1939 as *Astral Projection* (Reprint, University Books Inc., 1962). The book consists solely of the author's personal experiences, striking in their similarities to what today, forty years later, Robert Crookall has discovered to be recurring patterns in these phenomena— patterns of which Fox could not have been aware. The basic fault of Fox's narrative is his incorrigible theosophical background, which taints his writing to the degree that sections of the book have become quite obscure and slightly unpalatable. Like most studies of an autobiographical nature, various methods are outlined to enforce the experience. Most of these conform to the standard "occult" lore of its period.

We now come to the work of Sylvan Muldoon (in conjunction with Hereward Carrington) whose work in many ways is more convincing than Fox in that (1) he was not programmed by any occult doctrines and (2) his book to which we refer, *Projection of the Astral Body* (Rider & Co., London, 1929), was evolved with the help of a competent psychical researcher.

Basically, the volume is a straight personal account. Like Fox,

Muldoon offers several methods for experimental exteriorization—some novel, others from previous sources. Hereward Carrington's function throughout the volume was to provide footnotes which point out characteristics developed independently by Muldoon, but which also correspond to traditional projection lore, and to provide a summary of the literature on the subject. This bibliography, which was first printed in 1929, is now inadequate. Muldoon and Carrington's second cooperative venture was *Phenomena of Astral Projection* (Rider & Co., 1951), also of a semiautobiographical scheme, but with several other cases of reference. The book was somewhat haphazardly reviewed by Emanuel Schwartz in the *Journal* A.S.P.R., Volume XLVI, Number 4.

A study often referred to (for example, by Crookall, Smith, and Shirley) is, in its English translation from the original French, *Practical Astral Projection* by Yram (pseudonym) (Rider & Co.). Unfortunately, even more than Fox, the author was influenced by the occult thought which pervaded France at the turn of the twentieth century, and it is hard for the critical reader to determine what are actual out-of-the-body phenomena, and what is but Yram's imagination and fancy. In any event, the value of the book is enhanced by its similarities to Crookall's "patterns," which may be used as a sure standard in these matters.

The most recent autobiographical book on out-of-the-body travel is by Professor J. H. M. Whiteman, college professor, scholar, and mystic, whose effort *The Mystical Life* (Faber & Faber, Ltd., 1961) is a personal memoir of projection experiences. Unfortunately, the book is hard going for the layman, but it offers much insight into the mystical nature of out-of-the-body experiences and is a book well worth consulting. Robert Crookall has reviewed it in *Light*, Spring, 1963.

Of lesser note, and much earlier vintage, is Cora Richmond's *My Experiments out of the Body* (1876), which is now out of print and unavailable in the United States.

French Literature

Our newly unveiled concepts of the "fluidic double" were greatly determined by the continental parapsychologists in the early years of organized research. Of these, the French were the most active, since they were an outgrowth of the Mesmeric school of the psychic "fluid." One of the pioneers of French fluidic thought was Albert de Rochas, and it is a great loss that none of his books, all of which incorporate the doctrine of the "double," have found their way into English rendition.

A vastly distinguished study of the fluidic double is H. Durville's *Le Fantome des Vivants* (Paris, 1890) which, like the work of De Rochas, cannot be found in English translation.

One work which has been reprinted in English, though unfortunately abridged, is Gabriel Delanne's *L'Ame Est Immortelle*, which was translated by H. A. Dallas as *Evidence for a Future Life* (G. P. Putnam's Sons, 1904). Much of Delanne's case material is a rehash of *Phantasms of the Living* by Gurney, Podmore, and Myers (Kegan Paul, 1886), though a considerable amount of space is devoted to earlier French research, notably that of De Rochas. Several of Delanne's themes, principally the relationship of the "double" to the physical phenomena of mediumship and "astral matter," are more fully developed by Robert Crookall.

A huge French treatise on astral projection as an independent and self-contained phenomenon is Charles Lancelin's *Methodes de Dédoublement Personnel,* which appeared in France sometime before 1920. Like his predecessors, Lancelin's writing is lost to the English-speaking public. After summarizing the work of Delanne, De Rochas, and other French fluidists, he elaborated in detail upon them. At that time much of underground French occultism was focused on astral projection, but Lancelin's volume was the first to bring it before the academic community. A fair, though much abridged, recapitulation of Lancelin's volume may be found in Hereward Carrington's *Modern Psychical Phenomena* (American Universities Publishing Co., 1920).

The Work of Robert Crookall

For a total evaluation of the data on out-of-the-body travel we must turn to the books of Dr. Robert Crookall, which at this writing comprise eight volumes. They have a crucial bearing on astral projection.

Crookall's first complete volume *The Supreme Adventure* (James Clarke & Co., Ltd., 1961) was published under the auspices of the Churches' Fellowship for Psychical Study. The volume, a grand index of post-mortem communications from both scientific and spiritualistic literature outlines what the "dead" themselves have to say about the experience of dying. The full relationship of this study to astral projection is not fully seen until viewed in the light of his complementary second book, *The Study and Practice of Astral Projection*. Here we can see dramatically that the death experience as explained by the "communicators" is one and the same with the experiences described by those having spontaneous out-of-the-body experiences. This naturally has a crucial bearing on the survival enigma.

The strong survivalistic element of out-of-the-body travel is no better illustrated than in Crookall's *Techniques of Astral Projection* (Aquarian Press, London, 1964). The major attraction of the book is the commentary on "spirit teachings" received through the medium, Mrs. Keeler, whom Professor James Hyslop had sponsored as genuine. These teachings, mostly concerning the astral body and its exteriorization, were published in 1916. Crookall shows that her "communications" were far more advanced than any data known about the phenomenon at that time by psychical research. These include, among other features, data on the "silver cord extension" not developed until Muldoon's book some years later, and the fact that enforced projections differ from natural ones, not proved until 1964 when it was presented by Crookall in his books *More Astral Projections* and the *Techniques of Astral Projection*. Also noted are the experiments of Prescott Hall, who succeeded in producing out-of-the-body experiences by following the Keeler "communications." Further information in this short book includes deathbed observations, techniques of astral projection, and so on.

Another lengthy essay of the same year by Dr. Crookall is *During Sleep* (Theosophical Publishing House, Ltd., 1964), which

163

elaborates upon an old occult doctrine—that many of us project naturally during sleep to communicate with the "dead" and help them in their endeavor to assist others to project or pass through the death transition. The five complementary sections of the book comprise statements of astral projectors, psychics, deathbed observers, "communicators," and the views of psychical researchers. The material is all highly concordant.

Some of Dr. Crookall's concepts presented in this book and *Techniques of Astral Projection* are criticized by Professor Whiteman in *Light*, Summer, 1966; and are countered in the next issue by, among others, Raymond Bayless. Whiteman replies to his critics in the same issue.

Crookall's *Intimations of Immortality* (James Clarke & Co., Ltd., London, 1965) was published under the auspices of the Churches' Fellowship for Psychical (now) and Spiritual Studies. The first section of this slim treatise concerns astral projection and its relation to the survival issue. (Crookall is now working on another study devoted to more mass case presentations tentatively titled *Astral Projection and Survival* which is likely to be an extension of this present book.)

Crookall's theoretical treatise *The Next World—and the Next* (Theosophical Publishing House, Ltd., 1966) is an outgrowth of much of *Supreme Adventure* and *Study and Practice of Astral Projection* as they present the relationship of astral projection to apparitional observation. The study sets forth Crookall's explanation of the old problem of "ghostly clothing" which he theorizes to be a product of the "vehicle of vitality," which is the density factor of the astral body (corresponding to the "astral shell" of the occultists). The second part of the study is an extension of *The Supreme Adventure.*

Crookall's most remarkable and encyclopedic work is his recent *Events on the Threshold of the After-Life* (Darshana International, Moradabad, 1967), which is a grand recapitulation and tying together of all his previous books, and one that Crookall worked on for several years. The book is comprised basically of the inter-corroborative data presented by projectors, clairvoyants' deathbed observations, and the like. They in turn comment on the "birth" of the double from the physical body, the appearance of the newly born double, the nature of the "silver-cord extension," dual-consciousness, the return of the double to the physical body. A supplement is provided showing the similarities of this information as it is received from those "still in the flesh" and as it comes from mediumistic "communications." A second section of this lengthy book is dedicated to the exact experiences of the exteriorization phenomenon (similar to what Crookall formerly did with the death experience in *The Supreme Adventure*). Finally, various implications of this knowledge are discussed, including the concept of the objective "double" and its relationship to the physical phenomena of mediumship.

A fragmental, but harsh, review of this volume by Peter Maddeley was printed in the *Journal* S.P.R., Volume 44, Number 735, and is the subject of a reply by Crookall in the *Journal* S.P.R., Volume 44, Number 737 (see Appendix A).

Literature of Philosophical and Religious Traditions,
and the Concept of the "Subtle Body"

There is a woeful lack of authoritative literature concerning the concept of the "subtle body," in primitive religious and early philosophical thought.

One of the few studies, and an excellent one, of this nature is G. R. S. Mead's *The Doctrine of the Subtle Body in Western Tradition*, which was published in 1919 (Reprinted, paperback, Quest Books, Theosophical Publishing House, 1967). The short study, hardly more than a lengthy essay, traces the concept of the subtle body in Hellenistic, Platonic, and early Christian thought. It is remarkable how the concepts embodied in the book's second chapter, "The Spirit Body," are so closely similar to the data found in Crookall's work.

While no adequate single volume has been presented giving the role of the out-of-the-body experience in Eastern religion, there are scattered references to the subject in Crookall; and I have presented a study of astral projection and Tantric Buddhist thought as "Astral Projection in Tibetan Buddhist Literature" in the *International Journal of Parapsychology*, Volume X, Number 3.

Susy Smith devotes some space to primitive culture and out-of-the-body concepts in her previously mentioned, *The Enigma of out of Body Travel*. Professor Mircea Eliade has given some strikingly familiar concepts of out-of-the-body travel (though Professor Eliade has no conception of the psychical nature of them) and actual cases in *Shamanism* (Pantheon Books, 1963), and a few more in his book *The Sacred and the Profane* (Harcourt, Brace & Co., 1959).

In passing, we may also note some experiments in out-of-the-body travel according to cabalistic doctrines, by Walter Paul in *Light*, Spring, 1968.

Occult Literature

Since the medieval occultists had a highly developed doctrine of astral travel which they incorporated into their cosmology, some of their writings have quite a bearing on current literature. Franz Hartmann's biography, *Paracelsus* (reprint, McCoy, 1945), is an excellent anthology of the medieval Swiss metaphysician's views. In a similar category is W. E. Waite's *Mysteries of Magic*.

More adaptable to our needs is theosophical literature, with its highly evolved concept of the "composite double" (the astral body and its etheric envelope), a feature expounded by Crookall. A short but adequate digest of theosophical views is presented by him in *The Study and Practice of Astral Projection*. A more lengthy composition is Charles Hallock's *Luminous Bodies*, a rarity, having not been reissued since the 20's. Any of C. W. Leadbeter's books contain some standard theosophical lore, and Annie Besant's *Man and His Bodies* is a fair guide to occult tradition.

Miscellaneous Writings

The most important of these is, of course, F. W. H. Myers's *Human Personality and Its Survival of Bodily Death* (University Books, Inc., reprint, 1961), which included various cases from

Phantasms of the Living (which should itself be referred to) and the early *Proceedings* of the Society for Psychical Research. The famous Wiltse projection case is recounted in S.P.R. *Proceedings*, Volume VIII.

Two additional autobiographical sketches which are of considerable interest are M. Gifford Shine's *Little Journeys into the Invisible*, and William Dudley Pelley's *Six Minutes in Eternity*. Capsules of these two booklets may be found in most of the standard literature.

Historically interesting, but of little practical value and of questionable authority, are the books of A. E. Powell.

Quite a few additional cases are printed in Charles Richet's *Thirty Years of Psychical Research* (Collins & Co., Ltd., 1923), but the most authoritative source for the phenomenon of "bilocation" is found in the books of Professor Ernesto Bozzano, few of which have been translated from the original Italian.

Periodical Literature—Historical

There being such a vast amount of writings in periodical literature I can only cite here a few of the more important references. The extremely interesting articles by Prescott Hall which have been drawn upon by Crookall and Muldoon appear in their original form as "Digest of Spirit Teachings Received through Mrs. Minnie E. Keeler," *Journal* A.S.P.R., Volume X, and "Experiments in Astral Projection," *Journal* A.S.P.R., Volume XII.

A now forgotten case of experimentally induced and collectively perceived exteriorizations of the "double" was recorded by Henry Hillers in his "Projection of the Etheric Body," *Journal* A.S.P.R., April, 1935.

Some very decisive experiments in photographing the "doubles" of animals (one of which was successful), in a laboratory setting were conducted by R. A. Watters, who recorded his results in three short papers which appeared in the *Journal* A.S.P.R.: "The Intra-Atomic Quantity" (February 1935); "Phantoms" (March, 1935); and "Sleep" (April, 1935).

In the *Annals of Psychic Science*, 1905, Albert de Rochas presents some hypnotic age-regression experiments which incorporate the exteriorization of the double.

Eugene Osty in *Revue Metapsychique* (May-June, 1930) offers a considerable discussion of the phenomenon.

Periodical Literature—Current

The current surge of studies of out-of-the-body experiences in parapsychological periodical literature is due to the great influence of Professor Hornell Hart. One of his earliest contributions was a lengthy study *"ESP Projection: Spontaneous Cases and the Experimental Method"* in the *Journal* A.S.P.R., Volume XLVIII, Number 4, 1958. Hart's three conclusions were that hypnosis should be employed to induce the out-of-the-body experience (which had already been done by the early French fluidists),[4] that experiments should be devised with an agent (the out-of-body traveler) and a target individual to see if the agent could be perceived as an apparition (some cases of this were recorded in *Phantasms of the Living*), and that ESP projection could be experimentally controlled.

Hart further suggested various ways in which hypnosis could be utilized experimentally in the design of out-of-body research, and asked for a collection of case histories. This call was answered by Crookall a decade later. One of Hart's strongest summonses was for a psychological study of persons having such experiences. (Work on this level is now being conducted by Dr. Charles Tart, of the University of California at Davis.)

Hart's concepts were further evaluated in a paper "Travelling ESP" printed in the *Proceedings* of the First International Conference of Parapsychological Studies, 1955.

A year later Hart and his collaborators presented "Six Theories about Apparitions," a monumental study which may be found in the

---

4 The French fluidic experiments are not beyond reproach. Refer, for example, to G. C. Barnard's *The Supernormal* (London, Rider & Co., 1933).

Proceedings S.P.R. Volume L, 1956, in which it is shown that apparitions of the living (ostensibly, out-of-the-body experiences) and apparitions of the dead share common traits. Seeing that Hart chose a quasimaterial hypothesis to explain apparitional phenomena (and went a step further with his "persona" theory), the implications for the out-of-the-body experience are immense.

Hart uses the data of out-of-the-body travel as a strong argument for survival after bodily death in "A Chasm Needs to Be Bridged," *Journal* A.S.P.R., Volume LX, 1966, based to a great extent on Crookall's work.

His last contribution to parapsychological literature before his death was "Scientific Survival Research" (*International Journal of Parapsychology*, 1967), which recaps "Six Theories about Apparitions" and challenges anti-survivalists with the data collected and classified by Robert Crookall.

Still on a highly sophisticated level is Margaret Eastman's "Out-of-the-Body Experiences," published in the *Proceedings* S.P.R., Volume LIII. This cautious paper accepts neutrality in the objectivity of the phenomena but fails to note the work of Crookall, which was just beginning to be known at that time. Crookall counters Eastman's paper in *Light*, Summer, 1966, in his "Only Psychology Fact?"

On a more mystical level are the frequent periodical contributions of J. H. M. Whiteman, whose book *The Mystical Life* has already been discussed. Professor Whiteman's evaluation of many of the experiences he discussed, in the second chapter of his book, was published as a long paper in the *Proceedings* S.P.R., Volume LX, 1956. A more recent paper, and one of a theoretical nature, was "Evidence of Survival from 'Other World' Experiences," *Journal* A.S.P.R., Volume LIX, No. 2, which was a part of the Roll Survival Symposium and included several other papers printed in successive issues of that journal. The title of the paper is a bit of a misnomer, the actual theme is a plea for clarification of our knowledge of "other-world" experiences (in which he included experiences out of the body) and its relationship to the survival enigma.

Robert Crookall, who has so often been referred to, has issued several papers—some lengthy, some economical—in periodical literature. Many of these have been published in the College of Psychic Science's quarterly, *Light*.

Crookall has summarized the concepts he put forth in *The Study and Practice of Astral Projection* in the Winter, 1961, *Light* in an article, "The Reality of the Astral Body." For those interested in a more quantitative approach to the phenomena, "Statistical Tests of Astral Projection" is recommended (*Light*, Summer, 1966).

An important report citing evidence of the objective reality of the "double" and its ability to produce telekinetic effects is given by Mr. Lucien Landau in "An Unusual Out-of-the-Body Experience," Journal S.P.R., Volume XLII, No. 717.

Of a more experimental disposition are two epoch-making papers by Dr. Charles Tart: "A Psychophysiological Study of Out-of-the-Body Experiences in a Selected Subject," *Journal* A.S.P.R., Volume LXII, No. 1, and "A Confirmatory Psychophysiological Study of Out-of-the-Body Experiences in a Selected Subject," *International Journal of Parapsychology*, 1967.

The experiments upon which Tart reports are two EEG tests on subjects claiming the ability to produce the out-of-the-body state. Both of Tart's papers are successful in that curious data were recorded. But Tart does not cope adequately with the inconsistencies within his own experimental findings and has, in the former paper, pointed out his own experimental flaws. The application of psychophysiological testings to the experiences has been criticized by Crookall at the start of his book *Intimations of Immortality*.

This completes a survey of the more prominent literature available to us today. It is hoped that this short study will enable laymen and researchers alike to compile a comprehensive bibliography. It is especially critical that the inquirer have a ready index to guide him toward the scientific literature of a subject that has had so much popular rendition—this is crucial if parapsychology as a scientific discipline is to develop.

ACKNOWLEDGMENTS

The author is indebted for the use of copyright extracts which have been reprinted in this book by special permission of the following authors and publishers:

ABP International, Ltd., London (for Methuen Co., Ltd.)
Lodge, Sir Oliver: *Raymond*, 1916.
American Society for Psychical Research, N. Y.
Journal: Vol. X, 1916.
Proceedings: 1925.
Aquarian Publications, Ltd., London
Butler, W. E.: *The Magician, His Training and Work*, 1967.
Burns, Oates & Washburn Co., Ltd., London (for Burns & Oates, Ltd.)
Thurston, Herbert: *The Physical Phenomena of Mysticism*, 1952.
Surprising Mystics, 1955.
Cassell & Co., Ltd., London
Hill, J. Arthur: *Man Is a Spirit*, 1918.
College of Psychic Science, London, for:
Light:
Issues of: October, 1881; January, 1893; April, 1900; Vol. XLVII, 1927; September, 1945; Summer, 1962.
L. S. A. Publications, Ltd.
Dallas, Helen: *Human Survival and Its Implications*, 1930.
Crookall, Dr. Robert: *The Study and Practice of Astral Projection*, Aquarian Press, London, 1961.
More Astral Projection, Aquarian Press, London, 1964.
Darshana International, Moradabad, India
Crookall, Robert: *Events on the Threshold of the After Life*, 1967.
David McKay Co., Inc., N. Y.
Englebert, Omer: *Lives of the Saints*, 1951.
E. P. Dutton & Co., Inc., N. Y.
Underhill, Evelyn: *Mysticism*, 1955.
Fate Magazine (Clark Publishing Co.), Highland Park, Ill.

171

Issues of: July, 1951; November-December, 1951; March, 1960; June, 1960; April, 1967; October, 1968.
G. P. Putnam's Sons, Inc., N. Y.
Doyle, Sir Arthur Conan: *Edge of the Unknown*, 1930.
George Allen & Unwin, Ltd., London
Randall, Edward: *The Dead Have Never Died*, 1918.
Sudre, René: *Treatise on Parapsychology*, 1960.
George C. Harrap & Co., Ltd., London
Price, Harry: *The End of Borley Rectory*, 1946.
Guideposts, Carmel, N. Y.
Issue of: October, 1963.
Hamlyn Publishing Group, Ltd., Feltham, Great Britain (for Country Life, Ltd.)
Price, Harry: *Poltergeist over England*, 1945.
Harper & Row, Inc., N. Y.
Knowles, David: *The English Mystical Tradition*, 1961.
Henry Regnery Co., Chicago
Thurston, Herbert: *Physical Phenomena of Mysticism*, 1952.
Surprising Mystics, 1955.
Home & Von Thal, Ltd., London
Dingwall, Eric: *Some Human Oddities*, 1947.
Hutchinson Publishing Group, Ltd., London, for:
Hutchinson & Co., Ltd:
Fitzsimmons, F. W.: *Opening the Psychic Door*, 1933.
Rider & Co., Ltd.:
Jacolliot, M.: *Occult Sciences in India*.
Sherwood, Jane: *The Psychic Bridge*.
Summers, Montague: *Witchcraft and Black Magic*, 1958.
Institute of Psychophysical Research, Oxford
Green, Celia: *Lucid Dreams*, Hamish Hamilton, Ltd., 1967.
Ivar Nichelson & Watson, Ltd., Red Hill, Great Britain
Cummins, Geraldine: *Beyond Human Personality*, 1935.
James Clarke & Co., Ltd., London
Crookall, Robert: *The Supreme Adventure*, 1961.
Jan Van Loewen, Ltd., London
Dixon-Smith, Roy: *New Light on Survival*, Rider & Co., 1952.
Macmillan Co., Ltd., London
Singh, Sandhu: *Visions of the Spirit World*, 1925.
Meredith Press, N. Y. (for The Century Co.)
Flammarion, Camille: *Death and Its Mystery*, 1921.
Hyslop, James: *Contact with the Other World*, 1919.
Muldoon, Sylvan: *The Case for Astral Projection*, Aries Press, Chicago, 1935.

172

Oxford University Press, London
  Evans-Wentz, W. Y.: *Tibetan Book of the Dead*, 1960 ed.
    Tibetan Yoga and Secret Doctrines, 1958.
Parrott, Ian: *The Music of "An Adventure,"* Regency Press, London, 1966.
Psychic Press, Ltd., London, for:
  Psychic News:
    Issues of: June 4, 1966; August 6, 1966.
  Psychic Book Club:
    Findlay, J. Arthur: *Where Two Worlds Meet*, 1951.
Rare Book Reprints, Nashville, Tenn.
  Ingram, W. V.: *Authenticated History of the Bell Witch*, 1961.
Radha Soami Satsang Beas, Punjab, India
  Johnson, Julian: *The Path of the Masters*, 1939.
Routledge & Kegan Paul, Ltd., London (for Kegan Paul Co.)
  Cornillier, Pierre-Emile: *Survival of the Soul*, 1921.
Smith, Susy: *The Enigma of out of Body Travel*, Garrett Publications,
  N. Y., 1965.
Society for Psychical Research, London
  Journal: Vol. V; Vol. VI; Vol. IX; Vol. XVII; Vol. XXXVI; Vol. XLI;
    Vol. XLIV, Nos. 735, 736.
  Proceedings: Vol. III; Vol. VI; Vol. IX; Vol. XI.
University Books Inc., New Hyde Park, N. Y.
  Crookall, Robert: *The Study and Practice of Astral Projection*, 1965.
  Jaffe, Aniela: *Apparitions and Precognition*, 1963.
  Myers, F. W. H.: *Human Personality and Its Survival of Bodily
    Death*, 1961.
  Prince, Walter F.: *Noted Witnesses for Psychic Occurrences*, 1963.
William Collins' Sons & Co., Ltd., London
  Thomas, C. Drayton: *Life beyond Death with Evidence*, 1928.

ADDITIONAL BIBLIOGRAPHY

Abbott,David. *Behind the Scenes with the Mediums*. Open Court Publish-
  ing Co., Chicago, 1916.
Adare, Lord (Earl of Dunraven). *Experiences in Spiritualism with D. D.
  Home*. Society for Psychical Research, London, 1924.
Aiyar, Narajanaswami (ed.). *Thirty Minor Upanishads*. Madras, 1914.
Angoff, Alan. "The Literature of Religion and Parapsychology," *Interna-
  tional Journal of Parapsychology*, Vol. VIII, No. 2, 1965.
Annals of Psychical Science, Vol. II, London, 1905.
Anonymous. *Letters from Lancelot*, Dunstan & Co., Ltd., London, 1931.

173

Barrett, Sir William. *Death-bed Visions.* Methuen Co., Ltd., London, 1926.

Bayless, Raymond. *Enigma of the Poltergeist.* Parker & Co., N.Y., 1967.

Bennett, Sir Ernest. *Apparitions and Haunted Houses.* Faber & Faber, Ltd., London, 1939.

Besant, Annie. *Man and His Bodies.* Theosophical Press, London, 1900.

Bird, Malcolm. *Margery, the Medium.* Small, Maynard & Co., Boston, 1925.

Bozzano, Ernesto. *A propos de l'Introduction à la Metapsychique.*

————. *Les Phenoménes de Hantise.* Alcan, Paris, 1920.

Carrington, Hereward. *Modern Psychical Phenomena.* American Universities Publishing Co., N. Y., 1920.

Census of Hallucination. Society for Psychical Research, London, 1894.

Clanny, Dr. Reid. *A Faithful Record of the Miraculous Case of Mary Jobson.* Monkwearmouth, 1841.

Collins, Abdy. *The Cheltenham Ghost.* Psychic Press, London, 1948.

Crookall, Robert. *The Techniques of Astral Projection.* Aquarian Press, London, 1964.

————. *During Sleep.* Theosophical Publishing House, London, 1964.

————. *Intimations of Immortality.* James Clarke, Ltd., London, 1965.

————. *The Next World—and the Next.* Theosophical Publishing House, London, 1966.

————. "The Reality of the Astral Body," *Light,* Winter, 1961.

————. "Only Psychology Fact," *Light,* Summer, 1966.

————. "Statistical Tests of Astral Projection," *Light,* Summer, 1966.

Crowe, Catherine. *The Night Side of Nature.* Routledge Co., London, 1848.

Daily Chronicle (Great Britain), May 4, 1905.

Delanne, Gabriel. *Evidence for a Future Life.* G. P. Putnam's Sons, N. Y., 1904.

Durville, H. *Le Fantome de Vivants.* Paris, 1909.

Eastman, Margaret. "Out-of-the Body Experiences," *Proceedings* S. P. R., Vol. LIII.

Eliade, Mircea. *The Sacred and the Profane.* Harcourt, Brace & Co., N.Y., 1959.

————. *Shamanism,* Pantheon Books, N. Y., 1963.

Fernie, A. L. *Not Silent, If Dead.* Fernie, London, 1890.

Fox, Oliver. *Astral Projection.* University Books Inc., New Hyde Park, N. Y., 1962.

Funk, Isaac K. *The Psychic Riddle.* Funk & Wagnalls, N. Y., 1907.

Gardner, E. (ed.). *Dialogues of St. Gregory.* London, 1911.

Green, Celia. *Out-of-the-Body Experiences.* Institute of Psychophysical Research, Oxford, 1968.

Grout, Donald J. *History of Western Music.* W. W. Norton & Co., N.Y., 1960.

Gurney, Edmund; Podmore, Frank; Myers, F. W. H. *Phantasms of the Living.* Kegan Paul, London, 1886.

Hallock, Charles. *Luminous Bodies.* 1906.

Hart, Hornell. *Enigma of Survival.* Charles C Thomas Co., Springfield, 1958.

————. "ESP Projection," *Journal* A.S.P.R., Vol. XLVIII, No. 4, 1958.

————. "A Chasm Needs to Be Bridged," *Journal* A.S.P.R., Vol. LX, No. 4.

————. "Six Theories about Apparitions," Proceedings S.P.R., Vol. L.

————. "Traveling ESP," *Proceedings* First International Conference of Parapsychological Studies, 1955.

————. "Scientific Survival Research," *International Journal of Parapsychology,* 1967.

Hartmann, Franz. *Paracelsus.* McCoy Co., N.Y., 1945.

Heslop, F. *Life Worth Living.* Charles Taylor Co., London, 1928.

Home, D. D. *Incidents in My Life.* A. J. Davis & Co., N.Y., 1864.

Lancelin, Charles. *Methodes de Dédoublement Personnel,* Paris.

Landau, Lucien. "An Unusual out-of-the-Body Experience," *Journal* S.P.R., Vol. XLII, No. 717.

Lang, Andrew. *Cock Lane and Common Sense.* Longmans, Green & Co., Ltd., London, 1894.

Mead, G. R. S. *The Doctrine of the Subtle Body in Western Tradition.* Quest Books, Wheaton, Ill., 1967.

Moberly, Anne; Jourdain, Eleanor. *An Adventure.* Faber & Faber, Ltd., London, 1948.

Muldoon, Sylvan; Carrington, Hereward. *Protection of the Astral Body,* Rider & Co., London, 1929.

————. *Phenomena of Astral Projection,* Rider & Co., London, 1951.

Omez, Reginald. *Psychical Phenomena,* Hawthorn Books, N.Y., 1958.

Osis, Karlis. *Deathbed Observations by Physicians and Nurses.* Parapsychology Foundation, Monograph No. 3, 1961.

Owen, Robert. *Footfalls on the Boundary of Another World.* Trubner Co., London, 1860.

Pelley, William Dudley. *Six Minutes in Eternity,* 1929.

Price, Harry. *The Most Haunted House in England.* Longmans, Green & Co., Ltd., London, 1941.

Report on Spiritualism of the Committee of the London Dialectical Society, Longmans Co., London, 1871.

175

Revue Metapsychique, 1930.

Richet, Charles. *Thirty Years of Psychical Research*, Macmillan Co., N.Y., 1923.

Richmond, Cora. *My Experiments out of the Body*, 1923.

Rogo, D. Scott. "Astral Projection in Tibetan Buddhist Literature," *International Journal of Parapsychology*, Vol. X, No. 3, 1968.

Salter, W. H. *Zoar*. Sidgwick & Jackson, London, 1961.

Shine, M. Gifford. *Little Journeys into the Invisible*.

Shirley, Ralph. *The Mystery of the Human Double*. University Books Inc., New Hyde Park, N.Y., 1965.

Stead, W. T. *Real Ghost Stories*. Review of Reviews, London, 1891.

————. *More Ghost Stories*. Review of Reviews, London, 1892.

Summers, Montague. *Physical Phenomena of Mysticism*. Rider & Co., London.

Tart, Charles. "A Psychophysiological Study of out-of-the-Body Experiences in a Selected Subject," *Journal* A.S.P.R., Vol. LXII, No. 1.

————. "A Confirmatory Psychophysiological Study of out-of-the-Body Experiences in a Selected Subject," *International Journal of Parapsychology*, 1967.

Thelmar, E. *The Maniac*, Rebman & Co., London, 1909.

Thomas, C. Drayton. *The Dawn beyond Death*. Lectures Universal Ltd., London.

————. *Life Beyond Death with Evidence*. Psychic Book Club, London, 1928.

Tubby, Gertrude. *James H. Hyslop—X, His Book*. York Printing Co., York, Pa., 1928.

Waite, W. E. *Mysteries of Magic*.

Whiteman, J. H. M. *The Mystical Life*. Faber & Faber, Ltd., London, 1961.

————. "Evidence of Survival from 'Other World' Experiences," *Journal* A.S.P.R., Vol. LIX, No. 2.

Wickland, Carl. *Gateway of Understanding*. Psychic Book Club, London.

Younghusband, Sir Francis. *Modern Mystics*. John Murray, London, 1935.

"Yram." *Practical Astral Projection*. Samuel Weiser, N.Y., n.d.

SPACE
115 fixed location

STATES
of HEARERS
(16)

DEATH
13

TYPES
Radio > 14

CPSIA information can be obtained at www.ICGtesting.com
Printed in the USA
BVOW080635111012

302639BV00002B/28/A

9 781933 665030